LEADERSHIP ...
BIBLICALLY SPEAKING

The Power of Principle-Based Leadership

DAVID COTTRELL

CornerStone ■

Cover design: Keith Crabtree
Book layout design: Defae Weaver

Unless otherwise indicated, all Scripture quotations are taken from the *HOLY BIBLE, NEW INTERNATIONAL VERSION®*, copyright © 1973, 1978, 1984, by International Bible Society. Used by permission of Zondervan Publishing House. All rights reserved.

Scripture quotations marked KJV are taken from the *Holy Bible*, King James Version.

Scripture quotations marked LB are taken from the Living Bible © by Tyndale House Publishers, Wheaton, Illinois. All rights reserved.

The "NIV" and "New International Version" trademarks are registered in the United States Patent and Trademark Office by International Bible Society. Use of either trademark requires the permission of International Bible Society.

Library of Congress Catalog Card Number: 98-93877
    Cottrell, R. David., 1953–
        Leadership . . . Biblically Speaking: The Power of Principle-Based
        Leadership/David Cottrell

Printed in the United States of America.

ISBN: 0-9658788-1-3

Published by: **CornerStone Leadership**
                P.O. Box 764087
                Dallas, Texas 75376
                1-888-789-LEAD

This book is dedicated to the pastors who helped shape my life:

John Bisagno

H. D. McCarty

Ken Story

Herb Pedersen

Bill White

And to the person who most influenced my life as my pastor, friend, mentor, and father:

Ralph Cottrell

And to all pastors who sacrifice their time, energy, and love to further the kingdom of God.

Respect those who work hard among you, who are over you in the Lord and who admonish you. Hold them in the highest regard in love because of their work.
— I Thessalonians 5:12-13

TABLE OF CONTENTS

JACUZZIS, LADDERS, AND THE CROSS

Whoever acknowledges me before men, I will also acknowledge him before my Father in heaven. But whoever disowns me before men, I will disown him before my Father in heaven.

— Matthew 10:32-33

I was a Jacuzzi Christian. When being a Christian was relaxing, warm, soothing, massaging, bubbling, and without risk, I led the charge. I felt at ease sitting and enjoying the warm jet streams of idle conversations when Christianity was being discussed. But when being an active Christian became uncomfortable, my response was normally one of conformity: "Hey, I am a Christian, but I am not one of those eccentrics." I believed in the power, love, and sovereignty of Jesus Christ, but if you wanted to see that side of me, you had to follow me on Sunday—not on Monday through Saturday.

By the world's standards I was successful, yet my life was empty. I was standing at the top of the corporate ladder with the cross hidden in my pocket when I suddenly discovered that my ladder was propped against the wrong building.

Hiding my cross was my lack of commitment and total dedication to fulfill my purpose in the terms of God's will. The building my ladder was propped against was made of pride, money, and possession: not faith, hope, and love. I was successful, yet miserable.

I knew the Bible said to take up my cross daily, but I was taking up the cross only when it was convenient and without personal exposure. I did not truly understand what *"For the wisdom of this world is foolishness in God's sight"*[1] meant.

While reading Patrick Morley's introduction in *The Seven Seasons of a Man's Life* I realized that I could make a difference in the lives of others. Morley spoke of the shortness of our life on earth and what we do with the time we have. If I live to be eighty, my tombstone will read 1953 – 2033. His question was, "What will you do with the dash?" Good question. This book is part of my answer.

I enjoyed teaching leadership qualities and strategies, so I started a company to do just that. CornerStone Leadership Institute was created to teach the interpersonal side of leadership to business leaders. The CornerStone programs are biblically based but not biblically expressed. My first book, *Birdies, Pars, Bogies: Leadership Lessons from the Links,* used golf as the metaphor to teach leadership. The book has been successful; however, it does not fulfill my need to express my commitment to Christ, nor does it take the cross out of my pocket to share my faith and experiences with others.

Since beginning CornerStone, I have felt led to write a book that would connect the leadership principles I teach to God's leadership examples in the Bible. My reaction to that call has been much the same as Moses' reaction to God's call of leadership—who am I to put this together? I am just a businessperson who loves God and believes the Bible is the guide for our whole life, business as well as spiritual. But I truly believe that God has used me to present these principles in a way that is easy for you to apply wherever you are.

The purpose of this book is to provide a blueprint for successful leadership based on biblical direction and to answer some fundamental questions faced by Christian leaders. What can Christian leaders do to provide an atmosphere for success in a world where success is judged by the worth of possessions you have accumulated? How can we spread the word and be driven by profits at the same time? How can we live for Jesus while working with people who ignore the teachings of Jesus? What are the fundamental leadership principles that cannot be compromised by a Christian leader? All of these questions are answered in the Bible and are addressed in this book.

These principles are self-evident, self-validating, enduring, and they work! I did not invent them. They are principles of human relations that are taught throughout the Bible. The Bible is timeless and speaks vividly to us today! While reading this book, you will discover that the leadership principles expressed in the Old and New Testaments are just as applicable today as in the time of Moses, David, Job, Jesus, Peter, and Paul. These principles apply to all leaders in business, church, school, and our homes. You will also read the testimonies of successful people who experience the same challenges that you experience at work, at home, and in other areas of life. They share how they carry the cross daily in their chosen profession and use their talents to witness for Christ.

Regardless of our titles or the professions we have chosen, we are all leaders. The basic definition of leadership is influencing others, and every action we take has an influence on other people. The Bible provides explicit direction on how we are to influence others: *"For we are God's workmanship, created in Christ Jesus to do good works, which God prepared in advance for us to do."*[2] Wherever we work or play, we are to be a positive influence on others.

Our Mission Field

The opportunity to witness for Christ in our chosen professions is far greater than the opportunities to witness within our church. With few exceptions, a Sunday morning congregation of a typical church will consist of 95 percent or more professing believers. Most Sunday night congregations will be 100 percent professing believers. However, on Monday at work, most Christians are surrounded by nonbelievers. In fact, a church staff will have personal contact with fewer nonbelievers in a year than their congregation will in a week ... or maybe a day. The Christian's mission field is the workplace, and all Christians are missionaries. Paul wrote in Ephesians 4:1, *"I urge you to live a life worthy of the calling you have received."* We are each presented with opportunities to share our faith, through our words and actions, outside the four walls of the church. Nothing is more important than reaching the souls of the people, no matter where we are.

The need for Christian leadership in our society is real and is the Christian leader's responsibility. Because the problems of today are moral, behavioral, and spiritual, America needs God-loving, Bible-based leaders who are dedicated followers of Jesus Christ. Our employees should not be led by leaders without principles, our children should not be led by the immorality they see on television, and our churches should not be led solely by the emphasis on finances. The principles you will discover in this book are simple yet powerful. Do not allow their simplicity to fool you. They are the principles God provided us, through His word, to be the successful, fully developed Christian leaders He wants us to be.

Ultimately, we all have to answer the same question Jesus asked Peter: *"What about you?"* He asked, *"Who do you say I am?"*[3] When we are able to unashamedly answer that question wherever we are and allow God to be in control twenty-four hours a day, seven days a week, then, and only then, can we can enjoy all the blessings from God.

Use this book as a guide to help you get out of your Jacuzzi, prop your ladder against the right building, get the cross out of your pocket, and serve Jesus!

> *If anyone would come after me, he must deny himself and take up his cross daily and follow me.*
> — *Luke 9:23*

CHAPTER ONE

THE CALL FOR LEADERSHIP

I have indeed seen the misery of my people in Egypt. I have heard them crying out because of their slave drivers, and I am concerned about their suffering.

— Exodus 3:7

So now I am sending you to Pharaoh to bring my people the Israelites out of Egypt.

— Exodus 3:10

God's call for Christian leaders today has the same urgency as His call to Moses more than 3,000 years ago. Even though our leadership positions may be different from that of Moses, America needs Christian leaders to make a difference in our businesses, churches, schools, and homes. Many Christians are hesitant to share the Good News of Christ because of the same reasons Moses was reluctant to lead the Israelites. They do not feel qualified or trained, or they are not willing to accept the risk. The result is that there is little or no difference between the Christian leader's actions and the non-Christian leader's actions.

Even though Moses was asked to respond to God's call to lead the Israelites out of the wilderness in about 1450 BC, the situation today is strikingly similar to that described in Exodus.[1] People are miserable, they are crying out, and God is concerned because He loves us. America needs integrity-based leaders! Recent surveys reveal the following about attitudes toward leaders:

- Only 14 percent of leaders are seen by their followers as people they would choose as role models.[2] Isn't that a tragedy? Just 14 percent see qualities evidenced in their leaders that they would like to emulate, but a positive role model is more important than any other single aspect of leadership.

- Less than 50 percent of followers trust their leaders.[3] Trust is a basic requirement for effective leadership. How do you follow someone you cannot trust? Without trust, you cannot have faith; without faith, you are limited to accomplishing only that which is obvious to all. Great achievements cannot happen without trust and faith in leaders.

- Sixty-one percent of business leaders do not exhibit appropriate managerial behavior.[4] Whether it is lack of communication, confusing direction, lack of recognition, sexual or verbal harassment, or simply not doing anything, six out of ten are not effective leaders. This circumstance is the result of incompetency, insufficient training, or lack of desire to be a leader.

- Forty percent of employees said their leaders do a poor job of solving problems.[5] The purpose of the leader is to clear a path for people to be successful in accomplishing a goal. If you can't solve problems, you can't effectively lead people.

- Fifty percent said their leaders tolerate poor performance too long.[6] People want to be a part of a winning team, yet one-half of those surveyed felt their teammates were hindering the team's performance. The team members want accountability, but their leaders do not have the courage to address the poor performance of individuals on the team.

- Forty percent of leaders are threatened by talented subordinates.[7] The leaders feel threatened because they do not have enough confidence in their ability to lead talented people. Not hiring talented people assures long-term failure. Effective leaders hire the most talented people. They search for people with high intellect, experience, and the right personality to help them accomplish their goals. R. H. Grant once said, "When you hire people who are smarter than you are, you prove you are smarter than they are."

People are demonstrating their dissatisfaction by being disloyal to their leaders and companies. Many have become free agents, saying, "I'll stay here until a better offer comes along." On the average, U.S. corporations now lose half their customers in five years, half their employees in four years, and half their investors in less than one year. Disloyalty at these rates stunts corporate performance by 25 to 50 percent.[8] The cost of recruiting, hiring, training, and the lengthening of the productivity curve is staggering.

Employees did not create the disloyalty problem; leadership created the problem. Investor turnover creates a constant "do it now" mentality. The present quarter's profit is the only measurement that appears to matter. This short-term focus creates long-term problems. The fastest way to show quick profit is to cut expenses, and the largest expenses are personnel. The new accepted way: cut people, cut training, increase profits, cash in, and move on to the next deal.

Acquisitions, mergers, layoffs, and cutbacks all hit the central nerve of trust. People who have been laid off will never again give blind loyalty to an employer. Survivors become unable to give blind loyalty to their employers, because they have witnessed what happened to their associates and know that it could happen to them. The employee's position is, "You use me, and I will use you." It is not possible to have optimal productivity from people who are disloyal and do not trust their employers.

In addition to the unrest created by mergers, layoffs, and cutbacks, front-line and mid-level managers are thrown into the affray without sufficient training or experience. Many companies spend more time, money, and resources developing a mission statement than they do in developing strong leaders. In fact, some spend more money framing the mission statement than they do in equipping their leaders to be successful.

Just as when God called Moses at the burning bush, people need God fearing leaders today.

"I have indeed seen the misery of my people in Egypt."

- *People Are Miserable.* Every day 50,000 people quit their jobs. Studies have shown that the majority quit because of interpersonal conflicts with leaders. They are not dissatisfied because they make too little money, work too many hours, or have poor benefit plans. They quit because their needs are not being met—they need leaders with vision, integrity, and accountability. People want their leaders to recognize the contributions they are making every day. Without biblically based leaders, people are miserable.

According to an executive study by J. C. Staehle,[9] there are seven principal causes of unrest among workers:

1. Failure to give credit for suggestions
2. Failure to correct grievances
3. Failure to encourage
4. Criticizing employees in front of other people
5. Failure to ask employees their opinions
6. Failure to inform employees of their progress
7. Favoritism

All seven of these reasons are the result of poor interpersonal skills and the rampant ego of leaders. Such egos do not allow leaders to admit that they need their people more than their people need them. Nothing destroys people or organizations more quickly than leaders with egos out of control. Biblically-based leadership is servant leadership and eliminates all seven causes of unrest.

"I have heard them crying out because of their slave drivers."

- *People Are Crying Out.* The stress experienced in all areas of life today is a reflection of people searching for the truth. Employees are frustrated and are likely to transfer their frustration to their associates. Students, even in the most affluent neighborhoods, are turning to alcohol and drugs to overcome feelings of inadequacy. Both employees and students know there is something greater beyond the current scorecard of money, possessions, designer clothes and clubs. People need Christ-like examples in their businesses, churches, schools, and families. Their cries are for leaders with integrity and trust; their desires are for leaders who lead by positive reinforcement and are Christian role models in all areas of their lives.

"I am concerned about their suffering."

- *God Is Concerned About Our Suffering.* There are at least two common denominators among all people. God loves all of us, and we all suffer. Many times we look at other people who we admire and assume they have no reason to suffer. In fact, we sometimes make it a personal goal to walk in their shoes. They have money, possessions, friends, influence, family, and everything else we think would eliminate our suffering. The fact is that no one is immune to pain and suffering. If you were able to walk in anyone else's shoes, you would find that the other person is afflicted by many of the same trials.

The question we must ask ourselves is, "Why am I suffering?" Are we suffering for the kingdom of God? Or are we suffering because we have made poor choices? How do we know? The answer comes with our relationship with God and where the focus is in our life.

King David suffered for the kingdom of God and also suffered because of his poor choices. David was God's chosen, anointed leader, yet he was not allowed to accept his leadership position but was instead cast out to scrounge for food and shelter. During that time, David was in "righteous suffering," suffering within God's direction. Then, much later in his life, when he seemed to have things going his way, his suffering was the result of his bad choices. David changed his focus from God's plan to his personal, worldly desires. The result of his selfish decisions was disastrous.

God does love us! To suffer for the cross is worthwhile, but to suffer for worldly goals is opposed to God's will and purpose.

The Price of Leadership

As with anything important, there is a price to be paid for effective leadership. Leaving your comfort zone, accepting additional responsibilities, and being held accountable for your actions and the actions of others are part of the price of leadership. Moses knew the price that God was asking him to pay. Can you imagine how Moses felt when he heard God say that he had chosen him to be the leader? "Me? Lead your people? Ha! I am just a shepherd. I am perfectly content to tend my father-in-law's flock. The sheep don't talk back. I get them where they need to go by using this staff, and they never complain. All my communication is to myself. I enjoy what I do. I am the consummate individual contributor. I just lead sheep. I don't want to take the risk of leading the people. I don't think I would be good at it, anyway." Moses could have gone on to say, "Now, I have got to be creative and talk God out of this calling. Maybe he will show mercy and release me from the responsibility of this leading-his-people concept."

Moses was no different from us. He had his comfort zone and was reluctant to take a risk. Leading the Israelites would mean a change, and change is uncomfortable. Moses used his creativity and expressed five lame excuses why he was not the person that God really needed to lead his people:[10]

- Moses said, **But, Lord, I Am Not Qualified**. Moses' first objection was, *"Who am I?"* He probably thought, "I am just a shepherd tending sheep for my father-in-law. I have never led people anywhere, and I am not qualified for that responsibility." Few leaders have accepted leadership positions without being overwhelmed and frightened by the responsibility. Without God's guidance and direction, none of us are qualified.

  God saw in Moses far more than Moses could see in himself. He answered Moses' objection with the simple statement: *"I will be with you."* Then God gave a vision of the end result: *"When you have brought the people out of Egypt, you will worship God on this mountain."* Moses may have answered, "When I have brought the people out of Egypt? Wait, I am not through with my argument. You have already overcome my first objection, and now you planted a vision that describes the result of my success as the leader of your people! I am not ready for this."

- Moses was ready with another excuse: **But, Lord, I Am Not Trained**. Moses said, *"What shall I tell them?"* Moses felt that he did not have the training to know which direction to lead. He failed to realize that God had been preparing him all of his life to be the leader. He had been an Egyptian prince with everything done for him. Now he was a shepherd, and he had no one to do anything for him. God answered his objection: *"Say I am who I am. I am sent me to you."* Once again God looked to the future and told Moses what would happen: *"The elders of Israel will listen to you."*

  If you are in God's will, He will provide for your needs, regardless of the training you have received, no matter where God is leading you.

- Moses' next strategy was to personalize the risk: **But, Lord, This Is a Risk for You and Me**. By this time Moses must have felt he was not getting anywhere in his quest to avoid the call to lead. He then tried to spread the risk of the decision to include God. *"What if they* *do not believe me or listen?"* He thought that he would look foolish and cause God to look foolish. God answered with undeniable proof that Moses was the right person for the job. He changed Moses' staff to a snake, made Moses' hand leprous, and restored both.

All changes in jobs, responsibilities, and business involve risks. These risks include looking foolish, making bad decisions, losing pride, and being held to a higher standard. There is far more exposure to risk for leaders than followers, but the greater risk is *not* following God's call for us. All Christians are commanded to be Christian leaders, regardless of their job titles or responsibilities. Refusing to respond to God's call will make them miserable until they accept the risk and trust God to provide.

- Then Moses delivered the excuse that he thought could not be overcome: **But, Lord, I Physically Can't Do It**. Moses was feeling the same way many people feel about the requirements of leadership. By accepting leadership positions, today's leaders may face excessive travel, confrontations with the media, an overwhelming number of speeches, continual relocations, and other personal hardships. Moses had another good reason—*"I am slow of speech and tongue."* You have to admit that this was a good excuse! Moses was not a good communicator, and he knew that good verbal communication is a basic requirement for strong leadership. You can imagine his uncomfortable feeling. He had been leading sheep! What kind of motivational speeches did sheep require?

Once again God provided the answer, but instead of healing Moses' slow tongue, God sent Aaron to be Moses' spokesman. Isn't it interesting that God chose to change a staff to a snake and make a hand leprous and restored, yet chose not to heal Moses' slowness of speech? Obviously, God could have made Moses an eloquent, strong communicator to lead His people. Instead, Moses was like all of us, with weaknesses that God used to make him a better person and leader. Aaron was chosen by God to supplement Moses' weakness. The lesson for today's leaders is the same: admit your weaknesses and surround yourself with talented employees who can complement your weaknesses. Putting the right team together is key to your leadership success.

- By this time Moses was desperate: **But, Lord, Please Send Someone Else**. He had used up all of his excuses, and God had overcome every obstacle. His last attempt was this appeal to God: *"O Lord, please send someone else to do it."* Moses was wanting someone else, anyone else, to be the chosen leader. He still was not confident that he could do the job, because he was looking at the challenge from his perspective. God was looking at Moses from a different perspective and was totally confident. He was probably fed up with Moses' excuses. God said to him, *"Take your staff and go!"* You are the man. You are God's man!

Moses was out of excuses. He resigned his shepherd job and obeyed the Lord! Look what happened. *"Moses and Aaron brought together all the elders of the Israelites, and Aaron told them everything the Lord said to Moses. He also performed the signs before the people, and they believed. And when they heard that the Lord was concerned about them and had seen their misery, they bowed down and worshipped."*[11]

Summary

God still calls leaders who are imperfect, unsure of themselves, untrained, afraid of failure, and unable to understand why God has called them to lead. God calls CEOs, vice presidents, supervisors, team leaders, individual contributors, schoolteachers, principals, students, husbands, wives, sons and daughters, pastors, and Sunday school teachers to be leaders. Wherever you are called to work, you are called to lead.

If you are waiting on perfect conditions before doing what needs to be done, you will never get anything done. The Bible says, *"Whoever*

watches the wind will not plant; whoever looks at the clouds will not reap."[12]
Don't wait on conditions to be perfect before you trust God's direction.

The following chapters will guide you through the principles of biblically based leadership and provide practical applications to use in your work. Accept the challenge and respond to the call for leadership in your chosen field.

No temptation has seized you except what is common to man. And God is faithful; he will not let you be tempted beyond what you can bear. But when you are tempted, he will also provide a way out so that you can stand up under it.
— I Corinthians 10:13

How Successful Leaders Carry the Cross

Ken Byrd
Vice President
Bank United

My walk with God begins with a discipline of spiritual and physical exercise. I begin each day with a quiet time with the Lord, followed by jogging with a friend. During my quiet time I use two short devotionals and then pray. I enjoy this time, and it is vital to my healthy Christian life. Every day I pray specifically for five or six Christian brothers that are facing the realities of running small businesses.

I am subtle in my witness at work. I never say I am lucky; I say I am blessed. I treat everyone as the golden rule teaches. My peers know I am a Christian, and I share with them when the opportunity presents itself. I will not sacrifice my integrity for any deal and pass on anything that conflicts with my beliefs. I know to whom I am ultimately accountable.

THE POWER OF PRINCIPLE - BASED LEADERSHIP

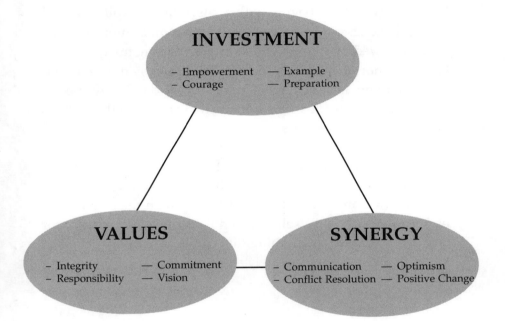

PRINCIPLES OF SUCCESSFUL LEADERSHIP

INVESTMENT

VALUES

SYNERGY

PART ONE

THE VALUES PRINCIPLES

INTEGRITY • RESPONSIBILITY • COMMITMENT • VISION

Everything begins with the values principles. Do I trust you? Will you allow me to accept my responsibility? Are you committed enough for me to risk my commitment? Do I know where we are going and why? These are all questions asked by your followers. If they are not answered positively, people will not follow. The values principles are the foundation of leadership.

CHAPTER TWO

INTEGRITY

My lips shall not speak wickedness, nor my tongue utter deceit.

— Job 27:4

THE PRINCIPLE OF INTEGRITY

Leadership results improve in proportion to the level of trust earned by the leader.

In a study of 1,300 senior executives, when asked which leadership trait—in a list of sixteen—has the single greatest impact in enhancing an executive's effectiveness, 71 percent listed integrity at the top.[1] Do you know how difficult it is to get executives to agree on anything— especially when there are fifteen other choices? Why is integrity such an obvious answer? The participants in that study know the same thing you and I know—if the leader has sacrificed his integrity, nothing else really matters. Does it matter how often you communicate with your people if they do not trust you? Most people will go entirely out of their way to avoid communicating with people whom they do not believe. Does it matter how committed you are, what mission statement you have developed and framed on the wall, how optimistic you are, how skilled you are at resolving conflicts, or how courageous you are if your followers do not trust you? None of those leadership traits really matter if your integrity is continually questioned by your followers. *Integrity is the cornerstone of leadership!*

People want to be led by leaders whose words are congruent with their actions, who have earned their followers' commitment and have proven to be honest and trustworthy. People want to follow leaders whose values are consistent and do not change based on the situation of the day. It sounds pretty simple, yet leaders' sacrifice of integrity is the principal reason why people lose faith in their leaders and look for someone else to follow. Judgment errors are forgiven and forgotten; integrity mistakes are always remembered.

What Is Integrity?

What is integrity, and how do you measure it? The dictionary says integrity is the rigid adherence to a code of behavior which can be measured only by a person's actions. Your spouse may say it is total commitment and loyalty. Your employees may say that it is doing what you say you will do. Your investors may define integrity as finding no surprises in your financials. Your friends probably say it is just being who you are.

Regardless of who describes it, integrity is a by-product of trust, which is a by-product of honesty. A deficiency of trust and honesty plagues many leaders today, costing companies millions of dollars in unrealized sales and profits. When people do not trust their leaders, productivity, job satisfaction, morale, turnover and company pride all are negatively affected. More important, the lack of integrity in Christian leaders causes nonbelievers to become skeptical and turn away from Christianity. God's standard for integrity in leaders is living a walk and talk that resemble the conduct of Jesus Christ. *Integrity is the principle leadership trait that influences positive results.* There is never a good reason to sacrifice your integrity!

Psalm 15 defines integrity and explains the results of a life of integrity. It reads: *"Lord, who may dwell in your sanctuary? Who may live on your holy hill? He whose walk is blameless and who does what is righteous, who speaks the truth from his heart and has no slander on his tongue, who does his neighbor no wrong and casts no slur on his fellowman, who despises a vile man but honors those who fear the Lord, who keeps his oath even when it hurts, who lends his money without usury and does not accept a bribe against the innocent. He who does these things will never be shaken."* Can you imagine the pleasure of working with people who fit the description in this passage? A blameless, righteous, truthful, honorable person who keeps his word even when it hurts is the type of person we would all like to be. It is also the type of leader people desire to follow.

The Bible describes many men that would not sacrifice their integrity even when it hurt:

- Jacob instructed Joseph's brothers to return the money they had mistakenly brought back from Egypt. Even though the money was not stolen, the message was clear—return what is not yours![2]

- Job's integrity was constantly challenged, and he withstood the test. Job knew that his code of behavior was to honor God, and he never wavered in that conviction. After losing his flock, Job blessed the name of the Lord. With such physical pain that even his friends did not recognize him, Job blessed the Lord. When his friends questioned his loyalty to God, Job honored God. Job never wavered in his integrity, and God blessed him many times over.[3]

- David spoke of integrity protecting him. In Psalm 25:21 he wrote, *"May integrity and uprightness protect me, because my hope is in you."* Integrity means that we are consistent in everything we do.

- Proverbs 19:1 compares our integrity with increasing our riches: *"Better a poor man whose walk is blameless than a fool whose lips are perverse."* In other words, it is better to give up everything than to lose integrity.

- Proverbs 21:3 tells us that keeping our integrity is more important than our rituals: *"To do what is right and just is more acceptable to the Lord than sacrifice."* Do what is right—that is the essence of integrity.

- Luke 16:10 teaches us that regardless of our wealth, our integrity should be consistent. *"Whoever can be trusted with very little can also be trusted with very much, and whoever is dishonest with very little will be dishonest with very much."* Integrity is not dependent upon how much you have—it is based on how you use what you have been given.

The Integrity Gap

The world's standard for integrity is completely different from God's standard. The Christian standard is do what is right regardless of the consequences. Paul wrote, *"Do not be overcome by evil, but overcome evil with good."*[4] The world's standard is to do what is right when it is convenient, or do what you want to if your chances for getting caught are negligible. Today's leaders must decide which side to choose; they cannot straddle the integrity gap.

Developing trust depends entirely upon the integrity you consistently demonstrate. Often times, leaders will spend more time polishing their image than protecting their integrity. They are more concerned about how they look or sound than about their actions. Who are they trying to fool? Leaders are ultimately judged on their actions, not their image.

Leadership can be compared to an iceberg. People see what is above the water—that is image and personality. Unseen is the much larger, greater, and more powerful foundation below the water level—this is your character and integrity. People are able to immediately judge leaders' personalities and images because that is what they see. Character and integrity can be judged *only* through trials and experiences.

Everybody's integrity is eventually tested. Before the test, you must decide the price you will pay to be a leader following God's standard of integrity. The greater your responsibilities, the more your integrity will be exposed. As you make decisions, you will be judged less on your image and more on your consistency of character. You should guard your integrity as you would guard your most valued treasures in a vault.

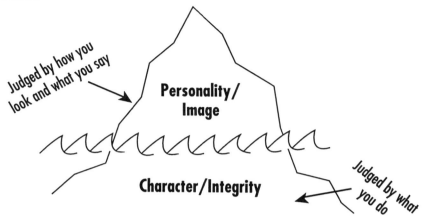

Integrity in the News

Recently, lack of integrity among our leaders has become so prevalent that we are calloused to the news. It has become accepted as the norm in everybody's eyes but God's.

Check out the news on any day:

- Campaign funds have been misappropriated and raised illegally.
- An evangelist goes to prison for income tax evasion.
- Investors are convicted of insider trading of company stock.
- A surprise witness confirms sexual abuse allegations.
- A major university declares 70 athletes ineligible and forfeits games.
- A popular movie is based on a lawyer having to tell the truth for 24 hours. Why is it so funny? Because we can relate to his uncomfortable situation.
- In Miami, nearly one in every three city workers has filed for workers' compensation or disability. One hundred and twenty-three workers received workers' compensation for falling out of or into

chairs; ninety were injured by desks; fifteen were sidelined by lifting a TV or watching television; seven were disabled by paper cuts and two by candy.[5]

- In one major city, the superintendent of schools, whose job was to protect and train our most precious resource, our children, pleaded guilty to embezzlement to avoid other charges. She embezzled taxpayers' dollars to furnish her house, losing her $200,000 job because she sacrificed her integrity for $16,000 worth of furniture. At her sentencing the judge stated, "You had this trust, and you violated that in a blatant way. It almost looks like an arrogant abuse of power." What a price to pay—the loss of everything that she had diligently worked for, including the trust of thousands of people. Such trust will not be given to the next superintendent for a long, long time.

Integrity Out of the News

It is easy to criticize these integrity mistakes. Before we cast our stones, however, we may want to check ourselves. Integrity mistakes happen all around us, and most of the time those integrity flaws do not make the news. Consider these situations:

- Padding the expense account to cover "miscellaneous expenses"
- Taking office supplies from work because "they overbought anyway"
- Making long-distance calls at work because "they can't track them"
- Stretching the truth to get an order
- Not returning phone calls
- Copying software from work to use at home
- Being "out of the office" when you are really in the office
- Using "I didn't receive the message" as an excuse to protect you from your lack of action

All of these actions are easily justified, appear to be minor, and, of course, "everybody does it." Yet they chip away at your integrity, and by example you are leading the people you influence to justify the same minor lies. The integrity question is: *When is a lie small enough that it doesn't matter?* Is there ever a time that dishonesty doesn't count?

Most people do not make a conscious decision to sacrifice their integrity by making one big, bad mistake. It is an accumulation of bad choices, all of which seem minor, that leads to the next bad choice. It builds without leaders being conscious of their loss, and ultimately you become immune to the situation.

One Degree at a Time

It is like the story of how to boil a frog. If you throw a frog into a pot of boiling water, he will leap out immediately because he knows that is not where he wants to be. Yet if you put the same frog in a pot of cold water and slowly turn up the heat, the frog will not recognize the subtle changes in temperature and will remain in the pot until he is cooked. He becomes complacent about the minor changes in temperature and is not conscious of his danger. That is how many people sacrifice integrity—one degree of dishonesty at a time—not even aware of the severity of their situation.

No matter how big or small a deal we justify to ourselves, God holds Christian leaders accountable to a standard of absolute integrity. The common denominator of many of the great Bible heroes was integrity. God knew that they could be trusted completely, regardless of the situation. Those great men were trusted to do what was right whether anyone was around or not. God expects the same from us, but keeping our integrity is a continual challenge for all Christians. Even the Apostle Paul wrestled with his integrity. See if this sounds familiar: *"For I have the desire to do what is good, but I cannot carry it out. For what I do is not the good I want to do; no, the evil I do not want to do—that I keep on doing."*[6] I am sure you can relate to Paul's struggle—we have all been there! The only way to consistently make the right choices in our lives is to have a deep, personal relationship with Jesus Christ and allow Him to help us make the right choices.

A leader without integrity who is followed because of his looks, a recent speech, or a charismatic personality is a leader who will be successful for only a short period of time. The leader who is consistent in his code of behavior over a long period of time will have committed followers. The Bible says, *"Blessed is the man who perseveres under trial, because when he has stood the test, he will receive the crown of life that God has promised to those that love him."*[7] Proverbs 10:9 says, *"The man of integrity walks securely, but he who takes crooked paths will be found out."* We cannot escape accountability in regard to our integrity.

Protecting Integrity

So how can we ensure we maintain our integrity? There are five pillars of integrity for the Christian leader, each is based on biblical values. Failure to adhere to any of the five will destroy your followers' confidence, their trust, and your leadership:

1. *Keep your promises and promise only what you can keep.* A mistake many leaders make is overcommitting or committing to something beyond their control. Living up to your commitments is one of the principal ways your integrity is judged. Your promises should involve only what you can completely control. Promising something outside of your control will place at risk your most precious leadership gem. Keep your promises to your followers and everyone else.

2. *Stand up and speak out for what you believe.* One of the greatest needs of all people and organizations is to clearly understand their core values. What is so important that it will never be compromised for any reason? When you answer that question the stress level of the entire organization will decrease while productivity and job satisfaction soar.

   Do not leave people guessing about how you feel. People are not mind readers. Understand exactly what you believe and communicate those beliefs without hesitation. If your beliefs and values are biblically based, they will not change. Know what your values are, commit to them, and let others know how you feel. The more you stand up and speak out for your beliefs, the more committed you become.

3. *Always err on the side of fairness.* When you are involved in a gray area, err on the side of fairness. What you do is being watched by all of your followers, and their judgments are made on *their* perception. They may not be fair, but you have to manage your people's perceptions. Not all decisions are black or white. If there is a gray area, make the decision that sides with your followers. Swallowing pride is a small price to pay to retain their trust in you.

4. *Live what you teach.* A leader who lives in conflict with his teachings automatically destroys his integrity and loses his ability to lead. People listen to what they hear you say and watch the way you deliver the message, but they react to what they see you do. You can't fake what you teach. If you don't believe it, don't teach it. Ralph Waldo Emerson said it best: "What you are speaks so loudly I cannot hear what you say." Walk your talk!

5. *Do what you say you will do.* The ultimate test of your integrity is whether you do what you say you will do. Your word and your commitment are judged every time you say you are going to do something—regardless of how insignificant you consider the commitment. In Matthew 5:37, Jesus taught us to *"Simply let your 'Yes' be 'Yes,' and your 'No' be 'No'; anything beyond this comes from the evil one."* Be reliable in honoring your commitments and promises. If the situation dictates a change and you are unable to live up to your word, communicate the reason thoroughly, honestly, and quickly to minimize the damage.

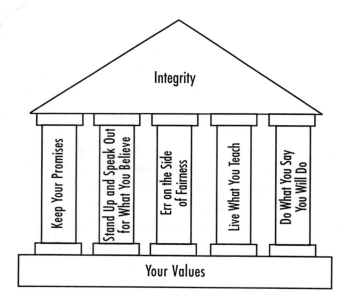

Protecting your integrity even involves protecting others' perceptions of you. Sometimes it is hard to accept that you are responsible for someone else's perceptions, but if you put yourself in a position to be questioned, you are putting your integrity at risk. The Bible says *"to abstain from all appearance of evil."*[8] Do not just abstain from evil—abstain from all appearance of evil. Although none of the following actions are immoral, they are easily questioned by others and may put you in a position to be questioned:

- Laying off employees while personally accepting a large bonus
- Taking business trips with your secretary
- Socializing outside work with an associate in a compromising place
- Creating a "business trip" with your family in an exotic location
- Meeting someone of the opposite sex alone over dinner
- Consistently working late alone with a business partner or colleague of the opposite sex

Obviously, some of those situations are business necessities. Just be careful. Paul instructed Titus not to even put himself in a position where his integrity could be questioned *"In everything set them an example by doing what is good. In your teaching show integrity, seriousness, and soundness of speech that cannot be condemned, so that those who oppose you may be ashamed because they have nothing bad to say about us."[9]* When your integrity is sacrificed or even questioned for any reason, there is a huge price to pay for its recovery. **People will forgive and forget judgement errors, but will not forget integrity mistakes.**

Business is personal. People commit themselves to other people, not to a company or organization. If people don't trust the messenger, they will not commit to the message. Leadership begins with the leader's integrity. Without integrity, you can't develop trust; without trust, you can't develop people; without developing people, you won't have followers; without followers, you have no one to lead.

INTEGRITY ➤ TRUST ➤ PEOPLE DEVELOPMENT ➤ FOLLOWERS = LEADERSHIP

Summary

Integrity is not just being fiscally trustworthy or handling issues in an exemplary and truthful fashion. Integrity is the commitment to do what is right regardless of the circumstance. No hidden agendas, no political games—do what is right! The Bible says, *"Even if you should suffer for what is right, you are blessed."[10]* If you take care of your integrity, your followers' trust in you will be sustained through the trials of your leadership. Protect your integrity like a priceless gem; it is your most precious leadership possession.

Hold yourself responsible for a higher standard than anybody else expects of you. Never excuse yourself.
—*Henry Ward Beecher*

How Successful Leaders Carry the Cross

Dr. Bob Griggs
Superintendent of Schools
Birdville ISD, Texas

I carry the cross primarily through my prayer life and by being an example for others to follow. I once had a Sunday school teacher who was a successful banker. He instilled in me the power of prayer in all circumstances. I have made prayer a major part of my life. I pray every chance I get throughout the day and make it a priority to find the time to pray. I pray in the shower, between conferences, and any quiet moment I can find.

I strongly believe the Lord put me in this job to be a positive example for others. I am certainly not adequate for the job, but several forces came together for me to be here. I know it was divine intervention.

My driving leadership principle is to always do the right thing.

Dr. Griggs was selected as Texas Superintendent of the Year by The American Association of School Administrators 1997, out of 1050 districts.

CHAPTER THREE

RESPONSIBILITY

From everyone who has been given much, much will be demanded; and from the one who has been entrusted with much, much more will be asked.

— *Luke 12:48*

THE PRINCIPLE OF RESPONSIBILITY

Leadership results improve dramatically when the leader and his followers accept total responsibility for their actions.

"Some assembly required." Oh, those are dreaded words that send chills up my spine. What they really mean to me is, "Some parts left over, frustration ahead, and you will never get it put together correctly. Ha, ha, ha."

When I have to assemble something like a bicycle, the typical scene goes like this: I open the box and place the parts all over the garage floor. I briefly glance at the instruction book; then I lay the book down because "I can figure this out." Several hours later, my task is completed. The bike is together, it rolls well, and I am proud of my accomplishment.

Then I discover that I have six nuts and bolts remaining. No big deal. I am sure someone made a mistake and simply packed too many nuts and bolts. I have never understood why there are always extra parts with the bicycle. I know I accomplished all that was required because my son, Michael, is riding the bike down the street. I am the man!

Several weeks later, the bike begins to wobble. I try to fix it, but I can't get the wheels to roll safely. Manufacturers just don't make bikes like they used to. This new, expensive bike has become just another piece of worthless metal taking up space in my already cramped garage. I blame the bicycle manufacturer for this outcome because I am sure there is no quality control in its assembly line.

I have a difficult time reminding myself that I am responsible for the bike not working properly. The six nuts and bolts I had remaining did make a difference. The person packing the parts did the job correctly and is probably a good worker. The manufacturer made a good product and had quality controls in all areas ... except making sure I followed the instructions. It is easy and sometimes satisfying to blame others, but the reason the bike doesn't work is that I did not assemble the bike properly. Once I accept that fact, I can quit blaming everyone else, stop making excuses, and learn from my mistake.

Sometimes responsibility is difficult to accept. Do you remember any time when you enjoyed hearing any of these statements? "It is not my fault." "If they had done what they said, I would have done what I was supposed to do." "I was too early." "I was too late." "I was too busy." "It was El Niño." Excuses are never scarce, but no one enjoys listening to excuses. They are unproductive, create negative emotions, and do nothing to solve any issue.

Making excuses and blaming other people or things rather than accepting responsibility for your actions are fatal to success. There are always excuses and others to blame for failures. Successful leaders avoid the temptation to fix the blame by searching for ways to solve problems. Accepting responsibility means looking toward the future; making excuses and blaming others focus on the past. To be an effective leader, accepting responsibility is not optional; it is mandatory. Being responsible leads to calmness, confidence, and self-control—all qualities of an effective leader.

When you accept your leadership position, you inherit the responsibility of being accountable for your actions and certain aspects of your followers' actions. Two of the truths of leadership is that *you always lead* and *everything you do counts.* You are not able to pick and choose what you want to count in your leadership. Everything counts! Your influence never goes away. You lead by what you do and you lead by what you do not do. No matter where you are, who you are with, or what you are doing, you are leading and someone is following. It's pretty scary, but every person you meet, know, and have known, and even those that know you only by reputation, are influenced through your actions. Successful leadership requires that choices be made based upon moral and spiritual considerations affecting both leaders and followers. It is your responsibility to use your influence to lead others in the direction they should be going.

The Bible is clear about our responsibility: *"Nothing in all creation is hidden from God's sight. Everything is uncovered and laid bare before the eyes of him to whom we must give account."*[1] Ultimately, we will have to account for the way we deal with our responsibilities in each area of our lives. We are responsible for our relationships with our families and work associates, our finances, and our health, and we are responsible for building the Kingdom of God.

Pilate chose to make no decision and attempted to transfer his responsibility to the Jews. Even though he did not say, "Crucify Him," his lack of action led to the crucifixion. He said, *"See to it yourselves,"* knowing what the people would do. He could not neglect his responsibility. The responsibility of Jesus' crucifixion lies with Pilate and the people, even though Pilate *"washed his hands"* of the situation.[2]

Jesus taught several lessons about responsibility through the parable of the loaned money.[3] In that parable, the master divided talents among his servants according to their abilities. Of the three men given talents, the man receiving the most talents accepted his responsibility, put the talents to work, and gained more. Another man was given fewer talents but accepted his responsibility and put his talents to work to gain more.

The third man dug a hole in the ground, hid his talent, and chose not to accept his responsibility of putting the talent to work. The two who accepted their responsibility were described as good and faithful. The one who did not was described as wicked and lazy, and he lost the talent he had been given. Regardless of our talents, we are all responsible for being good stewards of our God-given abilities and financial resources. The issue is not how much we have, but what we do with what we have.

Leadership Accountability

Along with accepting responsibility comes the realization that the leader's standard for accountability is at a higher level than that of his followers. James taught about the accountability of leadership: *"Not many of you should presume to be teachers, my brothers, because you know that we who teach will be judged more strictly."*[4] The same strict judgement of leaders applies today. The Christian leader whose sins are exposed has a far greater negative impact on others than a follower who commits the same sin. Everyone is ultimately held accountable for his actions, but the exposure of leaders' sin impacts the lives of more people. Well-known Christian leaders recently accused of embezzlement, greed, and adultery all had a negative impact on the cause of Christ because of the influence the exposure of their sins had on others.

In addition to a higher standard of accountability, many of the rights you might have claimed as a follower are lost as your responsibilities increase. You no longer have the right to blame others for mistakes—you are responsible. You no longer have the right to be negative or cynical—you are responsible. You no longer have the right to avoid issues and not solve problems—you are responsible. You no longer have the right to choose to not make a decision—you are responsible. **A leader's responsibility cannot be avoided!**

So what are you responsible for at work? The actions of your subordinates? Your boss? Your peers? The answer is that you are responsible for everything you control. You control setting the standards for your work group's performance, providing your subordinates feedback, solving employees' problems, giving your boss the positive or negative truth, providing input to your peers, and recognizing employees' accomplishments as often as possible. You control your choice of making excuses, complaining, or criticizing. You also control how much you build self esteem in others through sincere praise.

Most people go to work to do a good job. They perform at different levels, but they are there to do their best. Why, then, do their work results differ so much from their leaders' expectations? The former president of Hyatt Hotels stated, "If there is anything I have learned in my 27 years in the service industry, it is this: 99 percent of all employees want to do a good job. How they perform is simply a reflection of the one for whom they work."[5] In other words, the responsibility for the success of employees' results falls directly on the leader.

There are four major areas of a Christian leader's responsibility:

- Achieving results through others
- Creating and protecting quality time
- Creating a positive environment for success
- Obedience to God

ACHIEVING RESULTS THROUGH OTHERS

The leader's primary responsibility is to achieve results through the actions of others. If followers come to work to do a good job, why, then, are we surprised by their results? In Ferdinand Fournies' book, *Why Employees Don't Do What They Are Supposed to Do,*[6] Fournies cites ten reasons why your followers' results might be different from your expectations.

1. *They don't know what they are supposed to do.* A basic requirement of all followers is to know what they need to be doing to help accomplish the goal. The number-one stressor for employees is not knowing what the leader wants. Can you believe that? They are confused by ambiguity and inconsistencies on your part. Your role as a leader is to tell them exactly what is expected and let them do their job. If you leave your people confused about your expectations, don't act confused when they don't do what you expect.

2. *They don't know how to do it.* Putting people in a position without training is putting people in a position to fail. Many leaders assume their followers know how to do their jobs when in fact they do not know and are afraid to ask. How often have new managers been given the task of delivering performance reviews without being trained? How many times have employees been provided computers to improve their productivity but not trained to use them? Without providing the tools for your followers to be successful, they will not do what you want them to do. Ecclesiastes 10:10 says this about training: *"If the ax is dull and its edge unsharpened, more strength is needed but skill will bring success."* Do not limit your success by limiting your training budget.

3. *They don't know why they should be doing it.* People who do not understand why they should be doing a task think they have a logical reason not to do it. It is natural to respond better when they know why they are asked to do something. The "just do it" mentality does not motivate followers to get the job done. Sometimes the time constraints of explaining why in detail is burdensome but it is less burdensome, than losing the trust of followers because you did not fulfill their need to know why. No matter how often you talk about expectations, results will not come unless you clearly define the what and why of your expectations.

4. *There is no positive consequence for doing it.* Several times in this book the principle of *what you reward gets done* is reinforced. Many leaders feel that wages are the reward, but the positive consequence

most followers are searching for is personal recognition from their leaders. "Tell me that you appreciate the work I do" is their cry. Failure to communicate to your followers when they do a good job results in the loss of the opportunity to receive additional positive behavior. Reinforced positive behavior yields more positive behavior. Since most of your followers are doing what they are supposed to do, you have plenty of opportunities to reward them.

5. *They are rewarded for not doing it.* Why would anyone be rewarded for not doing what they are supposed to do? It happens all the time. People might work more slowly and be rewarded with overtime pay. People who complain about difficult tasks are given the easy tasks. Followers late to meetings are rewarded with a brief summary of what they missed while everyone else participated. Keep a close watch on what you are rewarding.

6. *There is no negative consequence for not doing it.* How many times have you heard people say, "Why does our company keep [him] around?" If there is no negative consequence of bad behavior or poor performance, you can't expect the bad behavior or poor performance to disappear. Followers must be held accountable for getting the job done, or the job will not get done. Someone once said, "The only day that everyone should be able to do whatever they want to do is their last day on the job." It is the leader's responsibility to hold people accountable for doing what they are supposed to do.

7. *They are punished for doing what they are supposed to do.* I can hear your thoughts. "That is ridiculous. Why would a leader do that?" See if any of these situations sound familiar:

- A person who does difficult tasks well is "rewarded" with more or all of the difficult tasks.
- A person delivering truthful but bad news is "rewarded" with verbal abuse.

- A person who suggests an improvement is "rewarded" with the extra load of the work to carry out his or her own suggestion.
- The best salesperson is "rewarded" with a disproportionate share of the quota.

These are just a few of the ways followers are punished for doing what we want them to do.

8. *They think they are doing what they are supposed to do.* Without the leader's feedback, people will make the assumption that they are doing what you want them to do. Your followers can be losing and think they are winning if you are not keeping score. The effective leader is the coach, referee, and scorekeeper. It is your responsibility to give frequent positive, negative, or neutral feedback. Consistent, frequent, and specific feedback will keep your followers from having to guess what you want them to do.

9. *They think something else is more important.* If you have not provided clear goals and expectations, you have left it up to your followers to decide what is important. That decision normally comes down to what is most comfortable for them. The burden of responsibility is on leaders to explain convincingly why what they want accomplished is important. If this is an area of concern in your work group, prioritize your requirements and hold your followers accountable.

10. *No one could do it.* Setting goals with unrealistic expectations will kill the morale of your followers. Goals have to be reasonable, attainable, easily understood, and worthwhile for your followers to be successful.

11. *You won't let them do it.* Fournies does not identify this reason, but many times I have witnessed the leader as the stumbling block. The environment you create in your work group will ultimately lead to the failure or success of your followers. An environment of open communication, respect, feedback, recognition, and continual

improvement will result in increased loyalty, decreased turnover, and increased profits. Keep an eye on what you are doing that might limit your followers' success.

Now, who is responsible for your followers doing what they are supposed to do? Clear direction, providing the tools, defining the purpose, positive rewards, accountability, continual communications, prioritization, and empowerment are all the ultimate responsibility of the leader!

Like it or not, you are responsible for your employees' results. Determine which of these reasons explain why you are not getting the results you expect. Then, make adjustments and go forward.

Puzzling Results? Check Yourself	Yes	No	I Don't Know
1. They know what they are supposed to do?	❑	❑	❑
2. They know how to do it?	❑	❑	❑
3. They know why they should do it?	❑	❑	❑
4. They are rewarded for doing it?	❑	❑	❑
5. They are rewarded for not doing it?	❑	❑	❑
6. There is a negative consequence for not doing it?	❑	❑	❑
7. They are punished for doing what they are supposed to do?	❑	❑	❑
8. They think they are doing it?	❑	❑	❑
9. They think something else is more important?	❑	❑	❑
10. They are capable of doing it?	❑	❑	❑
11. I allow them to do what they are supposed to do?	❑	❑	❑

CREATING AND PROTECTING QUALITY TIME

Another major responsibility of the leader is to create quality productive time for themselves and their followers. Effective time management is a major challenge. Interruptions and unproductive meetings are two major time robbers that create stress for leaders, steal their time, and inhibit their productivity. Taking control of those two areas will minimize stress and help you gain control of your time. Here are some ideas to help:

1. *Control Interruptions.* Every interruption requires three times the length of the interruption to regain lost productive time. In other words, twenty minutes of dedicated, uninterrupted time is more productive than sixty minutes of interrupted time. Here are some effective ways to control interruptions:

    — **Create dedicated blocks of time.** Dedicate time for decision making, administrative tasks, creative time for you, and time for your employees. Focused time is more productive than trying to do many tasks at once. The more activities completed in blocks of time, the more you will be able to accomplish in less time. You can gain 5, 10, or 20 minutes a day by improving your productivity through batching like activities.

    — **Manage your telephone.** The biggest single time-waster worldwide is telephone interruptions. You can control the management of your phone by following these simple steps. First, do all your callbacks at once. Choose a time that is least disruptive to your productivity and a time during which your employees will least likely need you. You will improve your productivity dramatically by doing all of your callbacks at a time when you are focused on the task. Second, avoid telephone tag by being specific as to when you will make callbacks or when you will be available for someone to call you back. Leaving a message to call without a specific time frustrates the person you are trying to reach, and the chances are slim that you will be available when they call. Third, when you leave a message, leave details about why you are calling, what can be done to prepare for your conversation, and when is the best time to return your call. The more information you provide on your message, the shorter your call will be when you do hook up with each other, which creates more time for you.

— **Another key to managing interruptions is to control drop-in visitors.** You know whom I am talking about—the person down the hall who wants to spend 30 minutes of his day with you making small talk. He walks away happy, and you are left with work to do that already should have been done. Drop-in interrupters can steal several hours per week from you that should be spent on something productive.

To take control of drop-in visitors and create additional time for yourself, try these tips:

- Create certain times of the day when you do not accept visitors. Put a "do not disturb" sign out. This could be catch-up time, think time or whatever your need might be. This suggestion does not apply to direct reports. When your employees need you, stop what you are doing and respond.

- Stand up when visitors come into your office. Don't let them get comfortable! Standing up sends a signal that your time is limited. Some executives even choose not to have chairs in their offices. If seating is needed, they go to the conference room. The amount of time your uninvited guests remains in your office is in direct proportion to their comfort level in your office.

- Politely tell visitors "one more thing before you have to go." You have taken control in regard to when the visit ends.

And if nothing else works—

- Show visitors something outside your office. Create a way to leave the office and don't let them back in—guard the door.

You can create additional time for yourself by controlling all interruptions! The better you work in blocks of time, manage your telephone, and control uninvited drop-in visitors, the more time you can spend doing what is important and productive.

2. *The second major time robber is unproductive meetings.* It is the leader's responsibility to make meetings productive. Meetings are necessary to facilitate communications but can be the most misused corporate resource. One of the largest expense items that does not appear on the income statement is meetings. Very seldom are people held accountable for the efficiency of their meetings. Ineffective meetings are a waste of time, money, energy, and emotions.

After years of evaluating meetings, these are my observations about most meetings:

- Most meetings do not have a definite purpose.
- Most meetings do not follow an agenda.
- Most meetings conclude without assignment of follow-up actions.
- Most meetings do not record any of the discussion.
- Most meetings include non-essential personnel, which load them up and reduce effectiveness.

In addition to the mismanagement of the logistics of meetings, once the meeting begins another group of meeting productivity killers arrive when the meeting begins:

- Most meetings are too long—participants would be able to accomplish twice as much in half the time if the meeting was properly managed.

- Eating where you are meeting is a productivity and time killer. Soft chairs and doughnuts will lengthen any meeting. Focus on the meeting, not on the menu.
- Most meetings spend more time on unrelated topics than they spend on the agenda topics. The typical meeting leader does not frame questions around issues to facilitate discussion.
- Most meetings are conducted without having all of the facts available to make good decisions.
- Most meetings have participants who do not tell the whole truth because they are afraid of what others will think of them.
- Most meetings end without anything happening. Why have a meeting if there is no resulting action? Ask the participants three hours after a meeting what was accomplished, and their responses may surprise you.

Meetings are a major expense. A four-hour meeting of twelve executives with an average salary of $75,000 costs about $1,800 in executive time. Is the meeting that you have planned worth $1,800? What will be the return on the investment? You are accountable to answer those questions before you call a meeting.

Here are some guidelines for creating productive meetings:

- *Have a good reason for calling a meeting.* If you don't have a good reason for the meeting, you have a good reason to cancel it. Your agenda, published prior to the meeting, should answer these three questions:

  - What is the purpose? All participants should know why they are there and what they're expected to contribute.
  - How much time are we investing in the meeting? Don't surprise people by meeting longer than expected. The minute you go beyond the expected time, the stress level rises and the attention level falls. Always plan your meeting to be completed well before your published time.

- What are we to accomplish? What are we to walk out of the meeting with? Participants need to know the specific goal of the meeting before they arrive.

- *Start and stop on time.* Your employees' time is their most important resource. If you do not honor their time, it is unlikely they will honor your time. If someone comes in late, never recap what has been covered. Continue the meeting and do not acknowledge the late arrival. By recapping the missed portion of the meeting, you are wasting everybody else's time, rewarding the person that was late, and punishing the people who were on time.

  One large, aggressive company has stand up meetings. Long before the meeting, the agenda is circulated, advising who is responsible for what. This approach allows everyone to be prepared. The meetings last about twenty minutes, and everyone is totally focused. No one can sleep through a meeting standing up. You can buy podiums for note-taking for far less money than the cost of one unproductive meeting.

- *Deal with the most important items first.* Get the most important tasks accomplished while the participants are fresh, and time constraints are not stressing people out. Never put yourself in a position to have to rush through your most important item or carry it over to the next meeting.

- *Summarize the results and clearly communicate the next step.* If no one is accountable for making the meetings productive, you have no chance to have productive meetings.

Meeting just to have meetings, shows a lack of responsibility on the part of the leader and is disrespectful to your employees. Here are six questions help you to evaluate your meetings:

Meeting Check	Yes	No
Do we have a good reason for the meeting?	❏	❏
Do the participants know the purpose?	❏	❏
Are we starting and stopping on time?	❏	❏
Do we deal with the most important items first?	❏	❏
Do we invite only the essential personnel?	❏	❏
Do we know what to do next?	❏	❏

If you answer no to any of those questions, you have not fulfulled your responsibility of honoring your employee's time.

CREATING A POSITIVE ENVIRONMENT FOR SUCCESS

Creating a winning atmosphere in your organization is also the responsibility of the leader. Just like the weather outside, the climate of your work group continually changes, and you must adjust to the change. The climate can allow for success or lead to failure. Your role is to create a climate that allows your followers to be successful and lets them be heroes to their customers. There are three critical facts about your organizational climate:

- *There is always a climate* in any organization. A climate always exists. The atmosphere you create will lead to success or failure.
- The *climate affects everybody* and everything. The climate in your organization affects all it touches, and it touches all. Some people may overcome the effects of the climate, but they still experience a definite climate.
- *You control the thermostat* by your actions. Everyone has an impact on the climate, but it is the leader's primary role. Most of the time you are aware of what you do to affect the climate. You are probably much less aware of when you do not do something to affect the climate. You can never not lead!

Effective leaders create a climate in which success can happen naturally. That climate is created through positive recognition, feedback for improvement, consistent communication, and empowering your employees to do their jobs.

Okay, I can hear you saying, "But my boss does not set a climate for success, so how can I?" I know exactly what you mean. I have been there. It is frustrating. Remember, your role as a Christian leader is to create a positive environment for your people and also create a positive relationship with your boss. Managing your relationship with your boss involves applying the same principles as leading your subordinates. What you control is your attitude and your actions. You cannot change his or her behavior but you can lead by example so that others might choose to change.

In *"The Seven Habits of Highly Effective People,"*[8] Stephen Covey wrote about the importance of understanding what you are concerned about and what you can influence. Things within your circle of concern are things over which you have no real control. Your circle of influence consists of things which you control. Focusing on your circle of influence expands the circle and decreases the energy you spend on things which are of concern but not within your control. The more you focus energy on what you influence, the more you are able to influence. When you accept responsibility for all you control, you have done your job. When the time is right, you will see positive changes happening outside your area of control!

OBEDIENCE TO GOD

As Christian leaders, we accept responsibility for our obedience to God. Regardless of the circumstance, we are responsible for others seeing Jesus in us and for living our commitment to Christ through our actions. This commitment is under our control. We should not be concerned about the reaction of others to our obedience to God.

Summary

When you accept your leadership role, a change in responsibility comes along with the change in title. You always lead, and everything you do counts. You are responsible for everything you control, including (1) knowing why your followers do not do what they are supposed to do, (2) the productive use of your time and your meetings, (3) creating a climate that allows your followers to be heroes, and (4) your obedience to God.

Enjoy taking responsibility, and you will enjoy greater results in all areas of your life.

> *One's philosophy is not best expressed in words; it's expressed in the choices one makes. In the long run we shape our lives and we shape ourselves. The process never ends until we die. And the choices we make are ultimately our responsibility.*
> —*Eleanor Roosevelt*

How Successful Leaders Carry the Cross

Clydene Johnson
Owner
Box Insurance Agency

I start every day with my quiet time with just me and the Lord. I work in an industry that is dominated by men and feel I need to be tougher, work harder, more forceful and more patient—all while I am carrying my cross. It is a challenge for me, and without my morning quiet time, it would be much more difficult.

My mom was a great example of how a strong Christian woman could take the spiritual leadership role in a family. My dad chose not to attend church, but Mom was faithful to make sure I was brought up with a strong Christian belief. I carry on that role in my family.

My spiritual gifts are patience and encouragement. My employees' balance in their life is important to me, and I work hard at treating them with dignity and respect. When anyone in my office makes a mistake, I take responsibility, fix the issue, and move on. My business is built on honesty and integrity, which I will not sacrifice for any reason.

Ms. Johnson is a member of the Grapevine, Texas, City Council.

CHAPTER FOUR

COMMITMENT

Whoever wants to be great among you must be your servant. And whoever wants to be greatest of all must be the slave of all.

— Mark 10:43-44 (LB)

THE PRINCIPLE OF COMMITMENT

Leadership results improve to the extent that the leader respects, recognizes, and develops his or her committed followers.

Having followers does not require skill. There are many people in leadership positions without vision, courage, integrity, optimism, or many of the other principles discussed in this book. They are leaders without leadership. Those leaders have followers because the people following them feel they have no other choice. A leader can pay people to follow, but money cannot buy *committed* followers. Committed followers exist only after the establishment of mutual trust between the leader and his people. The single greatest competitive advantage for a leader is to discover how to get the most of his people, especially when the leader is absent.

Committed followers understand the mission, commit to paying the price of success, and do what is necessary to accomplish the mission. Developing commitment requires a dedicated leader who recognizes, respects, and rewards his followers. Committed followership is the result of a committed leader who follows the leadership principles illustrated in the Bible.

When Moses was called to lead his people out of Egypt, both Moses and God knew that Moses could not do it alone. Moses had a weakness, being slow of speech, and God provided Aaron to cover that weakness. Moses could not have been as effective without Aaron, and Aaron certainly did not have the ability to lead by himself. Aaron was committed to do what was necessary to assist Moses in leading the people.

Moses also chose Joshua, a great strategist, who was totally committed to God and the mission. Joshua ultimately replaced Moses and played a key role in the exodus from Egypt. Joshua trained with Moses, his role model, until it was time for him to become the leader. He was prepared for his opportunity.

Jesus' Example

Jesus provided us with a blueprint for how to develop committed followers. Throughout His ministry, He consistently demonstrated three leadership qualities that separated Him from other leaders at that time:

- Jesus was compassionate toward His followers—He loved them and provided direction for them. *"When He saw the crowds, He had compassion on them, because they were harassed and helpless, like sheep without a shepherd."*[1] He cared for all of them regardless of their weaknesses and gave them hope for the future.
- Jesus met their individual needs—His followers came to Him with many needs: He ministered to the suffering, the lame, the blind, the crippled, and the hungry. He did what was necessary to meet their needs, and they were satisfied.[2]
- Jesus taught them—He taught them in ways that they could understand and relate to.[3] His message to His followers was clear.

Jesus also surrounded Himself with twelve disciples of different skills and abilities. Although several of the disciples' occupations are not known, we do know that some were fishermen, and Matthew was a tax collector. The disciples were ordinary men that Jesus allowed to become extraordinary. All of the disciples were great followers who led others to understand Jesus and contributed to the spreading of the Gospel.

Levels of Followership

Successful leaders today develop a team of subordinates with different talents to complement each other's strengths. They also understand that people are motivated for different reasons. Regardless of who the leader is, there are three levels of followers:

Three Levels of Followership

The first level includes those who follow because of necessity. This is the largest group. These people follow simply because they feel they have no choice. They feel threatened if they do not follow. They may be threatened by the loss of their jobs, changing their standard of living, losing their church affiliation, making bad grades, upsetting their spouse, or something else important to them. These followers are by far the most common and least effective. Once the threat, their only reason for following, goes away, they quit following. Threats create temporary responses, so their leaders must keep threatening to continue getting results. What an ineffective way to lead and what a miserable way to have to follow!

On the second level are people who follow because they have a desire to follow. They have an innate desire to accomplish a goal, regardless of the leader. Although there are fewer followers in this category than in the first one, this group is far more effective. These people are content to just do their jobs and are focused primarily on their activities, without concern for the overall goal.

The third level is the most effective group: followers committed to the leader and to the cause. These followers understand the mission, know the price involved, and will do whatever is necessary to accomplish the mission. They will run through walls to make it happen! Martin Luther King, Don Shula, and General Norman Schwarzkopf had committed followers. I know you have observed people who were able to earn commitment from their followers. While I worked at FedEx, I saw firsthand the impact of positive people working toward a common goal.

When Fred Smith created Federal Express, he was surrounded by a few committed followers. Not many people believed his concept would work. Their question was, "Why would you deliver a package from San Francisco to Los Angeles through Memphis?" His Yale professor gave him a C on the paper that he wrote explaining his idea. The investment community was not sold on the concept because they considered it illogical. Would you invest your money or career in such a radical concept? As Mark Twain said, "The man with a new idea is a crank until the idea succeeds." There were plenty of people calling Fred Smith a crank in the early '70s, but Fred Smith understood his mission, employed some committed followers, and in April 1973, FedEx became a reality.

You can imagine the excitement on the first night of operation! Fourteen FedEx planes in fourteen cities made their first midnight trip to Memphis. The packages were to be sorted and then reloaded to go to their city of destination. People were waiting to count the packages and celebrate their success. One by one they unloaded the planes. When all the packages were counted, there were twelve packages on the fourteen planes. How discouraging that must have been!

But, Fred Smith had committed followers. They understood the long-term mission and were committed to pay the price to make it successful. In fact, several pilots paid for their planes' fuel with personal credit cards to keep their planes in the air. Those were committed followers. Tonight, FedEx will sort and deliver more than three million packages. Revenues will be over $10 billion in 1998. More than 100,000 employees are on the payroll, thanks to the committed followership of a few special people, and the leadership of Fred Smith.

Your leverage to success is to increase the number of committed followers in your work group and decrease the number that are there only because of necessity. The greater the percentage of committed followers, the greater your chances for success.

Developing Committed Followers

There are four keys to developing committed followers:

- You must be committed.
- Surround yourself with talented people.
- Dehire your uncommitted and unproductive followers.
- Become a servant leader.

1. *You must be committed.* Before you can ask anyone to be a committed follower, you have to make the decision to be a committed leader. There is no middle ground to commitment. Jesus spoke to the church in Laodicea about indifference: *"I know your deeds, that you are neither cold nor hot. I wish you were either one or the other! So because you are lukewarm—neither hot nor cold—I am about to spit you out of my mouth."*[4] Everyone can understand Jesus' analogy. Drinking lukewarm water is disgusting! The committed Christian cannot follow Jesus halfway, and the Christian leader must be committed to those he is leading.

Commitment is action! Deciding to be committed and doing something about your commitment are entirely different. For instance, if three people were standing on the edge of a building and one person decided to jump, how many people would be left on the edge of the building? If you said three, you are right! Deciding to jump and actually jumping are different actions. Jumping requires commitment. Deciding to jump is a step toward action but does not require commitment. Leaders must do more than decide—they have to take action.

2. *The second key to commitment is to surround yourself with people who have talent to do the job and a desire to do the job right.* Picking the team is your most important function as a leader because your success rests primarily on the success of your followers. Nolan Richardson, head basketball coach at the University of Arkansas, enjoys sharing the wisdom of his grandmother and her impact on his life. One of the nuggets of wisdom she taught Coach Richardson was, "A great jockey can't win with a poor horse, but an average jockey can win with a good horse. Son, always get yourself a good horse." She knew the importance of surrounding yourself with talented people!

To accomplish any significant mission, you need talented and committed followers. If your team is made up of people who are not committed or talented, you will not be successful. Hiring talented people with different backgrounds and experiences creates diversity and increases your chances of understanding and solving your people's problems.

When Jesus was describing the body of Christ, He was teaching the value of diversity and synergy—where the whole is greater than the sum of the parts. *"God has combined the members of the body ... but that it's parts should have equal concern for each other. If one part suffers, every part suffers with it; if one part is honored, every part rejoices with it ... and in the church God has appointed ... apostles, prophets, teachers, workers of miracles, those having gifts of healing, those able to help others, administrators, and speakers."*[5] A successful team includes a variety of talents and experiences that a leader can use to make each member more effective with the team than alone.

- **Choosing the Right Team**

When choosing your team at work, select the people who have the skills and abilities to do the job and who also fit within your current organization. Formulate your interviews to discover the following about potential team members:

- Are their values congruent with yours?
- Do they bring additional talent to the group?
- Will they enjoy the company environment?
- Would you want your son or daughter to work with them?
- Would you invite them to your family table?

The way in which new people fit into the current situation is just as important as the skills they possess. A recent study of people who had been fired showed that only 30 percent of people were fired because of incompetence. The remaining 70 percent were fired because of interpersonal conflicts, lack of commitment, or incongruence of values.[6] Take time to make sure that new people will fit with your situation.

Your hiring decisions are more important than your management process. If you have the best management process with the wrong people in the job, your chances for success are not good. Hiring talented people is your leverage to success. Here is the formula for talent leverage:

$$T (R + E + C) = SUCCESS$$

Talent times (Reward System + Appropriate Expectations + Your Communications System) = Success. If you have a great management process in place, one that equals 9 on a scale of 10, but a person's talent is only 2 on a scale of 10, this is the result:

$$2 (9 + 9 + 9) = 54$$

If your management process needs improvement and is only a 3 on a scale of 10, but you are gifted at hiring talented people such as those who are an 8 on a scale of 10, note the difference:

$$8 (3 + 3 + 3) = 72$$

In the second example there is 33 percent greater efficiency than in the first, even though your management process is only one third as productive. Hiring talented people is your leverage to success. *If you learn only one management skill, learn how to find and hire talented people.* Hiring the right person is not easy. Most executives will hire fewer than five people a year. How good can you be at a process you complete only five times a year? It takes skill and patience to fill a position with the right person. Thomas Jefferson wrote to John Adams in a letter in 1823: "No duty the executive has to perform is so trying as to put the right person in the right place." The same letter could be written to any executive today.

An enemy of getting the right person in the right place is time. The pressure of "I have to have a warm body now" can rob you of your greatest performance leverage. Take your time. A mistake in the hiring process is one of the most costly mistakes you can make. Here are four tips to improve your chances for hiring successfully:

* *Use a well-documented decision analysis.* The decision analysis should identify all of the requirements of the job and weigh them according to their importance. When interviewing, ask the candidates questions that relate to the requirements of the job and score the candidates on their responses. At the end of your interviews, you will be able to objectively evaluate them without being influenced by things that are not important to their potential success.

Decision Analysis Example

Candidate _____

Date _____

Trait	Importance	x	Candidate's Evaluation 1=outstanding 5=unacceptable	=	Candidate's Score
Job Skills	1	x	_____	=	
Education	3	x	_____	=	
Attitude	1	x	_____	=	
Experience	2	x	_____	=	
Corporate Fit	1	x	_____	=	
References	2	x	_____	=	

Lowest total is most qualified

This decision analysis allows you to remove the personality from the decision and hire the person best qualified for the job. Understand the traits that you are seeking, objectively rate each candidate on those traits, and compare the results.

- *Follow the Rule of Three.* Interview at least three candidates for every position; interview your top two candidates three times and in three settings. The more information gathered in different settings, the better you will be able to evaluate their fit within your group.

Interviewing successfully is difficult because your interviewing skills are seldom used and your emotions are involved. Decisions are often made within the first four minutes of the interview and are based on irrelevant clues—a smile, firmness of handshake, or attire. It is not easy to make an unemotional hiring decision. According to one university study,[7] people make eleven decisions about us the first seven seconds of contact:

1. Educational level
2. Economic level
3. Perceived credibility, believability, competence, and honesty
4. Trustworthiness
5. Level of sophistication
6. Sex role identification
7. Level of success
8. Political background
9. Religious background
10. Ethnic background
11. Social/professional/sexual desirability

You have to look beyond these initial impressions to make a logical, long-lasting, successful decision. Do not make the mistake of choosing a person based on your "gut feel" or because they "appeared to fit in well." Get past those impressions and deal with the facts.

- *Hire the person knowing that you are seeing them at their very best!* You are seeing candidates on their very best behavior. Their smiles are the brightest; their attitude is the most positive; their appearance is their very best. If there is any conflict in how you think they fit with your corporate values, do not hire them! Many managers have been surprised to find that the person they hired on Friday looks and acts differently on Monday. Using a decision analysis and following the rule of three will decrease the chances of this surprise happening to you.

- *Pray for God's guidance.* Selecting the right team has the single greatest impact on your long-term success. Don't make that decision without praying for the wisdom to know who will be the best person for a position.

Take your time, find the most talented people for the job, and don't let them get away! Your new employees must be competent enough to reach their desired level of productivity quickly and fit well enough to remain with the company long enough to recoup the cost of hiring them. The most important activity you do is hiring the right person. Do it slowly; do it well.

3. In addition to being committed and surrounding yourself with talented people, you must *dehire the people who are not carrying their load.* Is that the Christian thing to do? Absolutely—if you have given them an opportunity to succeed and their performance is hindering others, it is the best course of action for the employee, your work group and you. If you choose to keep people who are not right for the job, you cannot be successful.

A person who is not right for the job and who creates a negative environment within the work group is like a cancer cell. A cancer cell turns against all other cells, and if it is not cut out completely, it will destroy the body. You cannot eliminate part of the cancer—it must all be removed. Negative, unproductive employees will destroy their work groups, every time. It is your responsibility to eliminate the barriers to your team's performance, and if you refuse to address the problem of an incompetent employee, you should wonder just who is incompetent.

The impact of keeping unproductive members on your team is illustrated by a golf experience of mine. I love golf and have discovered many leadership lessons from playing the game which I shared in *Birdies, Pars & Bogies: Leadership Lessons from the Links.* One of the most vivid lessons learned is the parallel of choosing the right equipment in golf and hiring the right employee at work.

For instance, I once bought a new club, a three wood, that was to be the answer to my game. It had the latest technology—titanium head, bubble shaft—and looked great! All of the golf magazines gave this club the highest ratings. I was proud of the purchase until I started hitting golf balls with the club. I hit hundreds of balls on the driving range and on the course. The ball just would not go where I wanted it to go when I hit the new club. You can imagine how frustrated I was. Finally, after an investment of $299, hours of practice, and many bad shots on the course, I had to make a decision: What am I going to do with this new club?

One of my alternatives was to leave the three wood in the bag and try to fool myself into thinking I had not made that mistake. The problem with the "ignore it" alternative was that I still needed a club to hit the distance of a three wood. The rules allow me to carry only fourteen clubs, so keeping the club I could not hit would prevent me from getting another club that I would trust and could hit consistently. Ignoring the problem was not a good choice.

Another alternative was to keep using the new three wood. Even after hundreds of bad hits, my pride was telling me that I could work it out. I tried one more round and was again rewarded with slices, hooks, rough, trees, sand, and out-of-bounds shots. Hitting this club was driving me crazy, hurting my game, killing my confidence, and affecting my attitude. Continuing to use the club was not the answer to my problem.

The alternative I chose was to accept the fact that this club was not right for me. Even though it was highly recommended and a great club for other golfers, it was not the right club for my game. I chose to accept my financial loss and loss of pride and sell it to someone more suited for the club. My friend who bought it from me (for $75) became a better golfer with the same club that was hurting my attitude, patience, and score.

Now I have a new three wood that I hit well and I feel confident hitting. The problem was not my swing or my club. The problem was that my swing was not right for that particular club. Once I reconciled the fact that I had done everything I could with the expensive, high-tech, good-looking club that did not work for me, I was able to improve my game.

The same lesson applies to your work. People who are not the best fit for your position will be an exact fit for someone else's position. The faster you act after making a decision to dehire, the better for you, your employee, and your work group.

Dehiring with Dignity

The single greatest demotivator of a team is to have members who are not carrying their load. It takes courage to let people go. Your emotions are involved, the employee's emotions and short-term livelihood are involved, and it is a tough conversation to have. If you have provided someone every opportunity for success, yet his performance fails to meet expectations, summon your courage and allow him to go where he can be successful. It is not a personal mistake of yours, nor is it a mistake of the employee—the job is just not right for him. Here are a few tips to help you dehire with dignity:

- Select the right time. When letting someone go, your concerns are for three groups of people—the person being fired, the work group, and you. It is best for all three groups for you to dehire in the morning. It provides an opportunity for the fired employee to gather his emotions and create a plan for a job search. It allows your work group time to get over the shock. And it saves you the stress of waiting all day to have the difficult conversation with the employee.

  Using the same logic, Monday is the best day and Fridays the worst day to dehire. A person let go on Monday can begin his job search the next day, and the work group has all week to recover from any shock caused by the firing.

- Do not hold out false hope. Many leaders put themselves in a bad situation by saying, "Let me think about it, and let's meet again tomorrow." If you have based the decision on facts, do not delay the inevitable because of your emotional involvement at the time of your delivery of the message. Be compassionate, but do not leave the meeting with the employee clinging to false hope.

- Be specific about your reasons why the job is not right for the employee. There should be no surprise if you have worked with the employee to correct deficiencies. Even though the dehiring should be expected, be prepared to express the reasons again during the dehire session.

- Settle money matters on the spot. If there is any gray area, err on the side of the employee. It is best to settle all outstanding issues before the employee leaves the premise.

- Never ...
  — Speak negatively about the employee.
  — Fire when you are angry.
  — Negotiate at firing.
  — Fire without the facts.
  — Blame someone else or the company.

  Be firm, be fair, protect the employee's self esteem at all costs, and wish him the best.

4. The fourth requirement to develop committed followers is for you to **become a servant leader.** Adopt Jesus' blueprint of caring for your followers, addressing their individual needs, and teaching them in ways they understand. Your role is to listen to their ideas, always treat them with respect even when their ways differ from yours, and provide direction for their success.

   Caring for your followers involves *serving* them rather than *using* them. Servant leaders know the value of their followers and are givers, not takers. Remember, you need your followers at least as much as they need you. Business leaders today describe this approach as the inverted pyramid. Leaders report to the people below them in the organization chart and ultimately to the customer.

Jesus is our example of servant leadership. He served others to the extent that He gave His life away. Jesus washed the feet of His disciples and told them that *"no master is greater than his servant."*[8] He was a servant to His followers.

Caring for your followers also involves recognizing and motivating them to make contributions. In my seminars, I ask participants to rank in order what motivates them. Out of hundreds of people, more than 80 percent say that recognition of accomplishment is the number one motivator. Not money, not benefits, not time off—just recognize me for what I do.

In a study by Howard Trien at Ford Motor Company, 5,000 workers and 7,000 supervisors were asked to rank ten values in terms of importance. The employees ranked the values in order of importance to them, and the supervisors ranked them according to how they believed the employees would rank them. Here are the results:

Values	5,000 Workers	7,000 Supervisors
Full appreciation of work done	1	6
Feeling "in" on things	2	8
Sympathetic help	3	10
Good wages	4	3
Good working conditions	5	4
Interesting work	6	1
Job security	7	5
Promotion and growth	8	2
Personal loyalty to workers	9	7
Tactful disciplining	10	9

Two facts immediately emerge from this study. First, the interpersonal side of leadership—being appreciated, asked for input, and supported by a person who cares—were all more important than money, promotion, and growth. This survey reinforces the fact that employees' sense of worth is more valuable than how much money they make.

Second, there was a huge gap between the perceptions of the supervisors and the priorities of the workers. How can you address people's needs when you do not know what is important to them? You may care, but unless you care about your followers' values, your people will perceive that you really do not care. Leaders who invest time and recognition in areas that are valued by followers are rewarded with improved productivity and greater job satisfaction.

Summary

Your success depends on developing committed followers and serving them. There is no scarcity of feet to wash. The only thing preventing us from developing committed followers is our lack of willingness to do what we ask others to do. Several years ago, research at North Carolina's Center for Creative Leadership identified the chief causes of executive failure in organizations. At the very top of their list were arrogance and insensitivity to other people. The next factor was betrayal of trust. Jesus warned us to control our egos, not to be arrogant, and to be sensitive to our followers. *"For everyone who exalts himself will be humbled, and he who humbles himself will be exalted."*[9] Successful leadership requires serving your followers.

You must make the decision to be committed, surround yourself with the very best people, dehire the people not contributing, and create an environment that supports your team's commitment. The ultimate test of leadership is what happens when the leader is not around. *There cannot be successful leadership without dedicated followership, and there cannot be dedicated followers without committed leaders.*

The best executive is the one who has sense enough to pick good people to do what needs to be done, and self restraint enough to keep from meddling with them while they do it.
—Theodore Roosevelt

THE CHRISTIAN LEADER'S COMMITMENT

It would not be right to leave a chapter dedicated to commitment without speaking about our commitment to Christ. The direction we have been provided is clear: *"Love the Lord your God with **all** your heart and with **all** your soul and with **all** your mind and with **all** your strength"*[10] (emphasis mine). That is total commitment—no lukewarm, no part-time, no halfway—total commitment to Christ. When we become totally committed, we can trust God that everything else will take care of itself.

Eugene Habecker suggested six evidences of intense commitment to Christ in his book *"Leading With a Follower's Heart."* [11] Here are his questions to check our commitment:

1. Do I live contrary to the ways of the world? *"Do not love the world or anything in the world. If anyone loves the world, the love of the Father is not in him."*[12]

2. Am I prepared to experience and/or suffer persecution? *"In fact, everyone who wants to live a godly life in Christ Jesus will be persecuted."*[13]

3. Do I place little value on material things? *"For where your treasure is, there your heart will be also."*[14]

4. Will I gladly and willingly surrender my personal rights? Christ is our example: *"Not my will, but yours be done."*[15]

5. Am I prepared to be involved in the lives of others? *"Carry each other's burdens, and in this way you will fulfill the law of Christ."*[16]

6. I am not ashamed of Christ and His words. *"If anyone is ashamed of me and my words in this adulterous and sinful generation, the Son of Man will be ashamed of him when he comes in his Father's glory with the holy angels."*[17]

When we can unequivocally answer yes to each of these questions, we will exhibit the total commitment Christ asks from us.

HOW SUCCESSFUL LEADERS CARRY THE CROSS

Dianne Gibson
Art Director
American Airlines

I am fortunate that my integrity and Christian values are seldom challenged at work. I feel strongly that God has put me where I am to witness for Him in all that I do. My Bible study and prayer life are important, but people judge me and the Christian life based on what I do. I feel it is important that we live what we learn and give nonbelievers a chance to see that you can be successful while living a Christian life!

At American, we have a Christian Resource Group. We meet together over brown bag lunches, have guest Christian speakers, and are able to share our faith openly in this forum. This has been a tremendous time for several hundred American employees.

My fellow workers see Jesus in me primarily by my humbling myself. I am learning to admit my mistakes, admit I don't know, ask for help and ask for forgiveness. This has helped me to put my faith in God, quit second guessing, and eliminate my fear to go forward.

CHAPTER FIVE

VISION

Where there is no vision, the people perish.

—Proverbs 29:18 (KJV)

THE PRINCIPLE OF VISION

Leadership results improve when leaders communicate a crystal clear vision and a convincing reason for accomplishing the vision.

Three people were working side by side on a construction job. When they were asked, "What is your job?", the first person replied, "My job is to do what I am told for eight hours so I can get a check." The second person said, "My job is to crush rocks." The third person replied, "My job is to help build a cathedral." Which of those three people do you think would be the most productive and the happiest and have the greater self-esteem? No doubt the third person, who understood that his job was far greater than just crushing rocks. He understood the vision and had a sense of purpose. His leader had focused on the result and communicated the vision in a way that the follower was able to concentrate on the cathedral while accomplishing the task at hand— crushing rocks.

Effective leaders have the ability to look where most people cannot see. They are able to see beyond the obvious and focus on something greater than the current situation. Outstanding leaders know where they are going and communicate the vision so that others will want to make the choice to follow.

Throughout the Old Testament, God provided direction and then presented a vision of the result of that direction. God told Abram, *"Leave your country and I will make you into a great nation, bless you, make your name great, and all people will be blessed through you."*[1] What a vision! That was certainly something greater than Abram's current situation.

God gave Moses a clear vision to *"bring my people, the Israelites, out of Egypt."*[2] Although Moses did not understand all the methods needed to make that happen or the challenges he would face, his mission was clear.

Joshua was given the vision to *"Be strong and courageous, because you will lead these people to inherit the land I swore to their forefathers to give them."* Joshua then passed the vision to his people—*"Consecrate yourselves, for tomorrow the Lord will do amazing things among you."*[3]

Jesus spoke of our spiritual vision. *"The eye is the lamp of the body. If your eyes are good, your whole body will be full of light. But if your eyes are bad, your whole body will be full of darkness. If then the light within you is darkness, how great is that darkness!"*[4] Jesus was speaking of our capacity to know what God wants from us and to keep our eyes focused on the goal.

When Jesus chose his disciples, His vision was clear: *"I will make you fishers of men."* From fishers of fish to fishers of men—they understood, for *"at once they left their nets and followed Him."*[5] They saw something greater than their current situation.

Jesus had a clear vision and sense of purpose for His ministry. He communicated that purpose in the synagogue in Nazareth: *"The spirit of the Lord is on me, because he has anointed me to preach good news to the poor. He has sent me to proclaim freedom for the prisoners and recovery of sight for the blind, to release the oppressed, to proclaim the year of the Lord's favor."*[6] He knew what He was to accomplish.

The disciples continually needed the vision reinforced to them by Jesus. Every time they were afraid, anxious, or confused, they lost the vision. Jesus constantly reinforced the disciples' purpose through his teachings as they walked with Him. Our followers are exactly the same—fear, anxiety, and confusion cause their vision to be blurred. Good decisions cannot be made under the stress of fear, anxiety, or confusion! *The leaders purpose is to calm the unrest, develop trust to eliminate anxiety, and give clear direction to eliminate confusion.*

A leader must deliver a vision that vividly explains how each person makes a difference, and one in which followers can see a worthwhile result. It must be a vision that generates energy, enthusiasm, and commitment among followers, a vision that clearly provides a consistency of purpose. As Peter Drucker says, "A monomaniac with a mission." If followers are concerned only with survival and have no sense of purpose, long-term results will not be satisfactory.

The "I Have A Dream" Vision

Martin Luther King was able to express his vision in a vivid, clear, moving way that generated energy, enthusiasm, and commitment from his followers. Listen to the vision he communicated in his famous "I Have A Dream" speech:

> *I say to you today, my friends, that in spite of the difficulties and frustration of the moment I still have a dream … I have a dream that one day in the red hills of Georgia the sons of former slaves and the sons of former slave owners will be able to sit down together at the table of brotherhood. I have a dream that one day even the state of Mississippi, a desert state sweltering with the heat of injustice and oppression, will be transformed into an oasis of freedom and justice. I have a dream that my four little children will one day live in a nation where they will not be judged by the color of their skin but by the content of their character. I have a dream … of that day when all of God's children, black men and white men, Jews and Gentiles,*

Protestants and Catholics, will be able to join hands and sing in the words of the old Negro spiritual, "Free at last! Free at last! Thank God almighty, we are free at last!"[7]

Martin Luther King's vision was clear, easily understood, and certainly focused on something greater than his current situation.

Developing Vision

How do you develop a vision? The *first* step is for you to be totally committed to the task. If you are serious about wanting to lead people, you must first be serious about leading yourself. Martin Luther King demonstrated his commitment through his activism—there was no question about his commitment. The lower your level of commitment, the more blurred your vision. You cannot fake commitment. Followers see through an uncommitted leader like a crystal glass. If you are not committed, don't try to be the leader.

Second, dream of the result. Martin Luther King dreamed of how things should be. If we overcome all obstacles, what is possible? A vivid vision of the result keeps everyone motivated. Not many people really understood Fred Smith's vision for Federal Express, but to Fred Smith the vision was vividly clear, and he never wavered in his communication to his followers.

Third, put your vision in writing. Does it lead exactly to where we need to go? Is it easily understood? Am I committed to doing whatever is necessary to accomplish the vision? A vision in writing becomes a mission, and once your mission is clear, you have accomplished one of the most difficult tasks of leadership.

Ultimately, your followers' ownership of the vision determines its success. You cannot afford to have your followers guessing about where you are headed. Chances are that they will guess wrong. Communicate often and consistently to all levels of the organization, and continually answer these four questions:

- *Is Our Mission Clearly Understood?* Your followers will provide desirable results only when they specifically know the mission, understand the mission, and are rewarded for the accomplishment of the mission. They have the right to know what is in it for them.

- *Do We Frequently Communicate How We Are Doing?* One of the basic needs of people is to know how they are doing and whether they are meeting expectations. This need is met through performance feedback, executive briefings, and communication of results. All communication should include the progress that has been made toward the accomplishment of the mission. If you are not communicating your mission and results every 15 to 30 days, you are not communicating enough. Keep the mission continually in front of your people.

- *Are We Rewarding What We Want?* Your recognition and reward system must accurately reflect what you are trying to accomplish. Check it out—you may be rewarding behavior that you do not want to happen. Many employees have been rewarded with an across-the-board raise when their individual performance actually hindered the performance of the work group. Make sure there is a positive consequence for a positive action and a negative consequence for a negative action.

- *Is Our Corporate Climate Contributing to Our Success?* Having a winning work environment—treating everyone with respect and dignity, listening to their concerns, and acting on their suggestions—will create winning results for your work group. Fred Smith said, "It is often not the mountain ahead but the grain of sand in the shoe that keeps us from reaching our goals." Take care of the small irritants and impediments to allow your followers to be successful.

Your ability to get others to see the vision and follow your direction depends upon your followers believing in you long before they invest in the vision. If you do not earn their trust, they will not accept your vision. Acceptance of your vision occurs long after their acceptance of you.

MISSION CHECK	Yes	No
Is our mission clearly understood by all?	❑	❑
Do we frequently communicate how we are doing?	❑	❑
Are we rewarding what we want?	❑	❑
Is our corporate climate contributing to our success?	❑	❑

How Followers Respond

Even though you clearly communicate the vision, have earned trust, and have commitment to the goal, not all followers will respond in the same manner.[8]

- *Some will never see the vision.* Their cry is, "Show me, show me, and then show me." They just can't grasp the result. They can still be good followers, but you will have to lead them with explicit directions to get them to go where you want them to go. They are very high maintenance, will drain you of your energy, and will keep you from spending time with your other employees.

- *Some will see the vision but just do not care.* This group is danger-ous. Their cry is, "So what?" They see what you are trying to accomplish but do not have the desire to pay the price to reach it. They are filled with apathy, and apathy is an enemy of success. This group is the least productive, and members of this group influence others to be less productive. You can train skills—you can't train desire. If you choose to keep these employees on your team, you have to be totally involved with them as you lead them to embrace the vision. If you have many followers in this category, your chance for success is minimal, and your chances of enjoying your job are even lower. These followers will keep you awake at night.

- *Some will see the vision and go after it.* Their battle cry is, "Yes, let's do it!" You empower them to accomplish the vision and let them go. These are great followers. They respond to positive reinforcement and positive leadership. Keep showing them the vision, and they will keep going after it. These followers will keep you motivated, and you will enjoy witnessing their accomplishments.

- *Some will see the vision and lead others toward it.* Their cry is, "Let's do it, and I will lead others to go with us!" You lead this important group through encouragement and then get out of their way and let them lead. These people are your most valuable asset. Your chances for success increase in proportion to the percentage of followers you have in this group. These followers challenge you to continue to improve and keep the vision refreshed. If your leadership only influences others to follow, your results are limited by what you can personally do. If you influence others to lead, then your results are unlimited.

Summary

People follow leaders who know where they are going. Only a fool would board a plane without knowing its destination. You should not expect people to follow without you communicating where you are going. *Excellent leadership vision does not necessarily guarantee excellent results, yet leadership without vision does guarantee failure.* Many leaders have a great vision but are not successful because they are unable to communicate the vision in a way that their followers can understand. If you effectively communicate, earn their trust, and remove obstacles, your followers will commit to the vision and pay the price to make the vision a reality.

> *Vision is the gift of seeing clearly what may be. Vision expands our horizons. The more we see, the more we can achieve; the grander our vision, the more glorious our accomplishment. The courage to follow our dreams is the first step toward destiny.*
> —Wynn Davis

HOW SUCCESSFUL LEADERS CARRY THE CROSS

Joe Miles
Sales Executive
Data Documents

I am aware that there has to be consistency in what I profess I believe and how I act. If an unbeliever cannot see consistency, it creates confusion of what it means to be a Christian.

In my business, developing long-term relationships is key to my success. My relationships are built on my integrity, knowledge of the industry, and my honest dealings with my customers. I work hard at developing trust, because people buy from people they trust. Regardless of the product, if they do not trust you, they will not buy.

My gift is being sensitive to others' feelings and the situation they are going through. I try to be different in my language and behavior to let others see Jesus in me.

THE VALUES PRINCIPLES CHECKUP

• Integrity   • Responsibility   • Commitment   • Vision

PERSONAL RATING   1 (low) — 5 (high)

1. I never sacrifice my integrity.   _____
2. I have earned my employees' trust.   _____
3. I accept responsibility for all I control.   _____
4. I control interruptions.   _____
5. I honor my followers' time.   _____
6. I conduct meetings that are productive and a good
    investment.   _____
7. I am confident enough to hire the best.   _____
8. I dehire employees who are not contributing.   _____
9. I communicate a crystal-clear vision for my followers.   _____
10. I accept that I am always leading.   _____
11. I enjoy the fact I am held to a higher level of accountability. _____
12. I am organized.   _____
13. I serve my followers.   _____
14. I am a good listener.   _____
15. My values are congruent with those in the Bible.   _____
16. I am committed to be a great leader.   _____

Three Areas I Commit to Improve:	My Actions to Improve
1.	1.
2.	2.
3.	3.

INVESTMENT

PRINCIPLES OF
SUCCESSFUL LEADERSHIP

VALUES — SYNERGY

PART TWO

THE SYNERGY PRINCIPLES

COMMUNICATION • CONFLICT RESOLUTION • OPTIMISM • POSITIVE CHANGE MANAGEMENT

Leaders who are able to relate to people from different backgrounds and create a winning atmosphere regardless of the situation are limited only by their own desire.

CHAPTER SIX

COMMUNICATION

Do not let unwholesome talk come out of your mouths, but only what is helpful for building others up according to their areas, that it may benefit those who listen.

— Ephesians 4:29

THE PRINCIPLE OF COMMUNICATION

Leadership results improve when followers understand their role and are rewarded for their accomplishments.

If you have seen Abbott and Costello's "Who's on First?" routine, you will probably remember the hilarious conversation between the two men. A baseball manager (Abbott) was telling Costello the names of his players: Who was on first, What was on second, I Don't Know was on third, Why was in left field, Because was in center, Tomorrow was the pitcher, and I Don't Give A Darn was the shortstop. The scene went like this:

Costello: So you're the manager. You know, I would like to know some of the guys' names so when I meet them at the ballpark, I'll be able to say hello.

Abbott: Sure, I will introduce you to the boys. They give them funny names, though, Lou.

Costello: I know. They give them all funny names.

Abbott: Let's see. Who is on first, What's on second, and I Don't Know is on third.

Costello:	(Interrupts) You the manager?
Abbott:	Yes.
Costello:	You know the guys' names?
Abbott:	I should.
Costello:	Then tell me the guys' names.
Abbott:	I said, "Who is on first, What's on second, I Don't Know is on third."
Costello:	(Interrupts) You the manager?
Abbott:	Yes.
Costello:	You know the guys' names?
Abbott:	I'm telling you their names.
Costello:	Then go ahead and tell me.
Abbott:	Who's on first.
Costello:	Who?
Abbott:	The guy on first.
Costello:	Who?
Abbott:	The guy on first. Who is on first.
Costello:	What are you asking me for? I am asking who is on first?
Abbott:	I'm telling you. Who is on first.
Costello:	You ain't telling me anything. I am asking who is on first.
Abbott:	That's right.
Costello:	Then go ahead and tell me.
Abbott:	Who.
Costello:	The guy on first base.
Abbott:	That's his name.
Costello:	Then go ahead and tell me.
Abbott:	That's the man's name.
Costello:	That's whose name?
Abbott:	Who is on first.
Costello:	What you are asking me for? I am asking you who is on first.
Abbott:	That's right. Who is on first.

And on and on Abbott and Costello "communicated" in furious agreement for eight more of the funniest minutes in the history of television. Have you ever felt as though you were in a "Who's on First" conversation where everyone was talking but no one was listening or understanding? Communication is more than talking. Communication means connecting with the other person's need to be understood.

The issue most often voiced in companies is, "Our company does not communicate." Employees become frustrated and feel they are out of the loop and no one really cares. Leadership becomes frustrated, saying "All we do is communicate; they just do not listen." Both sides could be right. Effective communication is a two-way exchange of ideas, methods, or reasoning that is understood by both parties. All followers have communication needs that must be addressed by their leaders. No matter how much you voice mail, e-mail, memo, or speak, if you are not addressing your followers' needs you are not communicating.

The ability to communicate effectively to people of different educational levels, backgrounds, and maturity is essential to a great leader. *Effective communication is the most important way to develop trust and commitment.* People will not follow leaders without fully understanding where they are going and why.

The Bible illustrates various methods of communication that were specific to the abilities of the followers to understand, comprehend, and act upon. Jesus chose to communicate through parables, often multiple parables with the same meaning. He knew that people could relate to the experiences of other people.

Through a fire in a bush, God called Moses to be the leader of his people.[1] When Moses saw the bush burning without being consumed, he wanted to investigate. Imagine being in the wilderness and seeing a bush burn but not burning up? The power of the Lord's communication was using the unexpected to get the attention of Moses.

Paul was a passionate communicator. Before his conversion, he was passionate in his persecution of Christians. After his conversion experience, Paul communicated the good news of Jesus with the same sincerity and passion. He was a great communicator because of his passion about what he was communicating. I imagine you could read Paul like a book, because he could not hide his passion and commitment. He is my favorite writer in the Bible.

Jesus was a consistent, faithful communicator to God. He made communication a priority and acted upon the direction given. He was a great listener, a requirement for effective leadership.

Jesus also communicated by touching people. He went where the people were in order to touch them, be with them, provide direction, and be empathetic to their needs. He communicated to them in their environment, where they were comfortable, and he treated them as individuals.

Barnabas communicated through his gift of encouragement. He encouraged Paul through Paul's early days as a Christian. Barnabas risked his life supporting Paul when others were skeptical of Paul's conversion. By encouraging Paul and Mark, Barnabas had a direct positive influence on the early Christian movement.

Communicating with Your Subordinates

Trust makes the greatest single impact on effective communication. People will go out of their way to avoid communicating with those they do not trust. Your first responsibility in communication is to earn the other party's trust and respect. Without trust, you are wasting each other's time.

Leaders must be creative in their communication and have a specific plan to communicate with different groups of people. The first group requiring effective communication is the people you are leading. Each person is motivated differently, creating unique demands upon the leader. The better you know your people, the more trust you will develop; and the better you communicate, the more effective your leadership.

Regardless of individual differences, followers have six basic communication needs that the leader must address. Notice how Jesus met each of these needs with His followers.

1. *All Followers Must Know "What Is Expected of Them?"* You would think that all employees would know their purpose at work; however, ambiguity about roles in the workplace is the major source of stress for employees. The following thoughts are typical in most companies:

   > *We provide them job descriptions and expectations. I just do not understand why they are not doing what they are supposed to be doing.*
   > —The Leader

   > *I just don't know what they want.*
   > —The Follower

   How frustrating for both parties. Leaders cannot understand why they won't do what they should be doing, and followers don't understand why leaders are not clear in what they want. They are frustrated over the same issue . . . their communication is not connected! What is required can be answered with job descriptions and job expectations, yet the real answer is communicated through your consistent message about your people's importance and purpose. The effective leader explains things personally and often. If a follower is wondering what is required of him, the chances of his doing what you want are not very good. Make sure every person knows exactly what you want. Be consistent, communicate often, and check for understanding. No matter how often you talk about what you expect, the desired results will not be achieved unless you clearly define the what and why of your expectations.

   Jesus was clear about what was required of His followers. His followers had to make a decision to resign from their lives of independence and submit to authority. *"If anyone would come after me, he must deny himself and take up his cross daily and follow me. For whoever wants to save his life will lose it, but whoever loses his life will save it."*[2] The expectations were clear, along with the reason why it was important.

2. ***All Followers Must Know How Their Leaders Think They Are Doing.***
Regardless of the maturity of your followers, they have to know how they are doing. The second major source of stress, after ambiguity of roles, occurs when the follower is unsure how he is doing, from the perspective of the leader. Employees can feel in control only of circumstances they understand and only when they know whether they are meeting expectations. The formal way to answer "How am I doing?" is through performance feedback and performance appraisal. However, if you answer this question only through formal methods, you will not address your followers' requirement to know more frequently. Everyone needs positive encouragement. Communicate frequently how your subordinates are doing. People are sensitive and desire to do a good job. It is human nature for people to want to know whether they are performing adequately or to be told what they can do to improve. The most effective encouragement is telling people how they are doing through positive feedback. It is the responsibility of the leader to catch people doing things right and reinforce that behavior.

The leadership style of Jesus was one of positive recognition and encouragement. God Himself praised Jesus at His baptism. *"And a voice came from heaven 'You are my Son whom I love; with you I am well pleased."*[3] The teachings of Jesus included servanthood, treating others with respect, and hope for the future. In the parable of the king's ten servants, Jesus used the example of the master praising the servant: *"Well done, my good servant."*[4] Positive feedback is a requirement for continued positive behavior.

Some guidelines for providing positive feedback:

* *Be sincere.* Giving positive feedback can backfire if it is not perceived as sincere. Most people are experts, or think they are,

at reading the sincerity of their leader. Faking positive feedback is risky. Be sincere, or wait until you can be sincere.

- *Be quick.* The sooner you give feedback after the behavior you are trying to reinforce, the better your results. If you give positive feedback only at performance review time or on other formal occasions, you miss a major leverage for improving productivity.

- *Give feedback often.* There is a significant difference in the perception of leaders and their followers as to how often positive feedback is given. In an extensive survey, managers were asked to respond to this statement: "I let my subordinates know when they are doing a good job." The subordinates responded to a similar statement: "My supervisor lets me know when I'm doing a good job." Same question, different perspective. The scale of 1 to 5 was used, where 1 = never and 5 = always.

The managers rated themselves a 4.3. The employees rated their managers a 2.3! That is a 200 percent difference in the amount of positive feedback managers believed they gave and the amount of positive feedback the employees felt they received. What a huge gap in perception![5] According to this study, every positive recognition receives only one half credit. Don't allow yourself to be fooled into thinking you recognize positive behavior too often. Do it twice as much as you think you should, and you will have a good chance of meeting people's needs.

Who was right or wrong in this survey is not the issue. The **perception** of the subordinates is what counts. Give positive feedback often!

3. *All Followers Must Know Whether Anyone Cares.* Whether you consciously answer it or not, the question "Does anyone care?" is always answered. The way to formally answer the question is through career development and a recognition program. Compassion and caring for your people, their sacrifices, and their

contributions are other ways the question is answered. The most effective way to show your followers you care is to invest your time in their development. The more you invest, the greater your return, but your investment must reflect what is important to your followers.

The more you praise employees for doing a good job, the better they will do and the more committed they will be to the mission. Here are several ways to show you care:

- Send thank-you notes to their homes.
- Recognize their company anniversaries.
- Have brown bag lunches and talk to them without the use of notes, scripts, or podiums.
- Memorize as many facts as you can about them—spouses' name, children, sports, etc., to demonstrate you care about them.
- Go to their offices and ask if they need anything from you.
- Send Thanksgiving cards.
- Personally hand them their paychecks and thank them.
- Never let a birthday pass without acknowledging this special day.
- Show them you care by spending time with them.
- Talk to them and act on their advice.
- Listen to them with empathy.
- Develop a habit of saying thank you.
- Make it clear that you appreciate them.

Jesus answered the question "Does anyone care?" with His leadership actions. He was an unselfish, compassionate, teacher who prepared His followers for additional responsibilities. Even with those actions showing He cared, He was still asked the question, "Don't you care?" at least twice in his ministry. The disciples, who had seen His miracles in person, questioned Him when they were afraid and in perceived danger. When they were in their boat during a storm, they woke Jesus with the question, *"Teacher, don't you care?"*[6] When Martha was frustrated because she perceived that she was having to do her sister's work, she asked *"Lord, don't you care?"*[7] If

Jesus had to answer this question, think how much more often we have to answer the same question for our followers. Our followers do not see us performing miracles; they see only our human mistakes.

"Don't you care?" has to be answered for your followers when there is change or when they are afraid, uncertain, or feel they are carrying too much of the load. You answer their question with your communication, actions, and compassion.

4. *All Followers Must Know How the Team Is Doing.* People want to be a part of a winning team and know that their contributions are worthwhile. Establishing work unit goals, team expectations, and feedback on the team's progress is essential to effective leadership. The more emphasis you can have on teamwork, the greater the accountability your team members will feel toward each other. Keep your followers informed about whether they are winning, or, if they are not winning, what they need to do to become winners.

Jesus was a team player. He believed in keeping peace on the team and having the team focused on the ultimate goal. When two of His team members, James and John, asked for preferential treatment and the remaining ten disciples became upset, Jesus called them together to settle them down and refocus their mission.[8] He reinforced the worthiness of their contributions and taught them that to be team players, they were to serve, not be served.

5. *All Followers Must Know Where They Fit in the Big Picture.* What are the company's goals, and what contribution does our team make toward its success? What is our impact on the total plan? Everyone needs to know their importance to the achievement of the overall goal.

Paul, on the road to Damascus, received clear direction on where he fit in God's plan and the result he was to expect. *"Now get up and stand on your feet. I have appeared to you to appoint you as a servant and as a witness of what you have seen and what I will show you . . . I am sending you to them to open their eyes and turn them from darkness to light, and from the power of Satan to God, so that they may receive forgiveness of sins and a place among those who are sanctified by faith in me."*[9]

Jesus let His disciples know exactly where they fit in the Master's plan and what roles they were to accept. He told them of the trials they would face, the price of following Him, and the false signs that would be before them. He told them everything in advance so that they would know where they fit in and would be prepared for their responsibilities.[10]

6. *All Followers Must Know How They Can Help.* What can we do to make a positive difference? What can we do to make our company better? Followers want to be a part of making a positive difference in the lives of others, and they need to know what they can do to make the difference.

When Jesus stated the great commission, He was clear in His instruction about what we are to do to help: *"Go and make disciples of all nations, baptizing them in the name of the Father, and of the Son and of the Holy Spirit, and teaching them to obey everything I have commanded you. And surely I am with you always to the very end of the age."*[11]

The responsibility of the leader is to address each of these six communication needs. If any of the needs are not being met, it is like rolling a wheel with a section of the wheel missing. You may arrive where you are trying to go, but it will not be a smooth trip. Be sensitive to each of these needs and create an ongoing plan to address each requirement.

Follower Communication Requirement Wheel

Keeping Focused

The responsibilities of leadership can be overwhelming at times. So many things come from different directions, making it difficult to separate the important from the trivial. One of the main responsibilities of the leader is to sort through what is not important and keep followers focused on the things that really matter.

Jesus was a master at keeping others focused. When Martha was so upset at Mary and questioned whether Jesus really cared, Jesus reminded her of what was important. *"Martha, Martha, you are worried and upset about many things, but only one thing is needed. Mary has chosen what is better and it will not be taken away from her."*[12] Jesus knew what was trivial and what was important, and he had Martha adjust her focus to the one thing that was important.

There are a few vital functions that determine your success. If the energy and direction of your people are being used on anything other than those vital functions, energy is being wasted. Your responsibility is to eliminate all of the nonessentials and to keep followers focused on the few vital, meaningful activities.

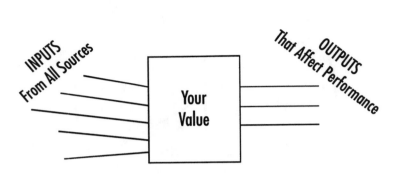

Peter Drucker said to always know the answer to these two questions: "What is our business?" and "How is business?" Your value as the leader is to provide clarity of purpose and consistently reward the accomplishment of the important few activities which affect performance.

Following are keys to focusing on the vital few:

- *Identify What Is Critical to Your Success.* Why do we exist? If we have the time or resources to do only three things, what would we be doing? What are the cost, the benefit, and the priorities of those vital few activities?

One of my favorite classic movies is *City Slickers.* As a typical baby boomer, I can relate to many scenes in the movie. My favorite character was Curly, a hard, crusty old man full of wisdom. His best advice to Mitch, who was experiencing mid-life questions, was in this scene:

Curly:	You all come out here about the same age. Same problems. Spend fifty weeks a year getting knots in your rope—then you think two weeks up here will untie them for you. None of you get it. Do you know what the secret of life is?
Mitch:	No, what?
Curly:	This. (Holds up his index finger.)
Mitch:	Your finger?
Curly:	One thing. Just one thing. You stick to that and everything else don't mean [anything].
Mitch:	That's great, but what's the one thing?
Curly:	That's what you've got to figure out.

Curly's "secret" is a personal relationship with Jesus Christ, but the same principle can be applied to your work group. Figure out what is important, spend your time and energy on the important items, and be the very best doing what you identified as being important.

- *Communicate What You Want.* After you figure out the critical success factors, clearly communicate them to your followers. Not knowing what is required is one of the main reasons people are unhappy at work. Involve your people in helping you identify their role in accomplishing your company goals. You provide the what and the why; let them tell you how.

- *Reward What You Want.* Your reward and recognition program must clearly reflect your goals. What gets rewarded will get done— make sure you are rewarding the right things. Never fail to acknowledge the positive behavior that will contribute to your success.

Consider two other points about communicating with your followers. *First*, over a two-week period, keep track of how often you communicate with each person and record the type of communication you have. Is it recognition/rapport: "Great job", or "What can I do to help?" Is it problem-solving? Is it telling your followers to do something or asking something from them? Or are you failing to communicate with them at all? *The greater percentage of time you spend recognizing positive performance and developing rapport with your followers, the better your long-term results.* If you always ask something of them or tell them to do something, you do not build a relationship that develops trust. Keep a record of your communications for two weeks. You will discover areas in which your communications can be improved.

Second, take the time to listen attentively to your followers. Alexander Pope once observed, "Some people never learn anything because they understand everything too soon." Two of the greatest obstacles hindering improvement in productivity are the leaders' egos and their inability or desire to listen. One of the deepest needs of all people is to be listened to and understood. A person who is genuinely interested in what others have to say will state his opinion only after listening to everyone else's opinion. Listening is the way you show how much you value other people and what they are saying, and is also the way to build trust.

Listening effectively is not easy. It requires three things that not many leaders have an abundance of: time, patience, and total concentration. As a leader, involved listening is an investment in your people. The better you listen, comprehend, and act upon recommendations, the more trust you earn from your followers. If you listen to hear only what you want to hear, you lose trust. Don't just sit there! Listen attentively, don't interrupt, wait a few seconds before replying, ask questions, and demonstrate you care by the attention you give. The best listeners make better decisions and become the best leaders.

Personal Contact and Communication

In the CornerStone seminars, we ask the participants to list the leadership characteristics of the most outstanding leader they know. The number-one characteristic is that the leader cares for them personally. Successful leaders care for their people and empathize with their needs. Just as in the time of Jesus, followers have a need for personal contact and communication on their turf. Jesus talked with people on all economic and social levels—the rich, poor, royal, hermits, lawyers, criminals, children, and adults. He met them where they were comfortable and addressed their needs. Many times He taught them while he was walking and/or eating, because the listeners were relaxed.

Today, being face to face with your followers and meeting with them on their turf require dedicated effort. Technology has been a great productivity enhancement in dealing with the technical side of management, but it has been a detriment to maintaining personal contact with your people. The explosion of e-mail and voice mail has shackled many leaders to their offices, their computers, or their phones.

In a recent *Dallas Morning News* article,[13] managers from a Dallas company were grumbling about getting more than 100 e-mails apiece every day. Eighty-four percent of those managers reported interruptions three or four times an hour. How productive can you be if you are interrupted this often and have 100 e-mails coming in every day? When one chief financial officer returned from vacation, he had 2,000 e-mails waiting. Can you imagine 2,000 e-mails? How long would it take to respond to 2,000 e-mails? It didn't take him very long. He chose to delete all of them and leave 2,000 people thinking they had communicated when in fact there had been no communication.

What a challenge today's leaders face to make it a priority to lead as Jesus led—by being in personal contact with followers. All people desire to know they are okay, and nothing replaces your personal communication of that message. A handshake and a look in the eyes to say thank you have a far greater impact than any message on a computer screen. It may seem strange, but the more you use technology in your communications, the more you will need to have face-to-face communication with your followers. Don't allow your online communications to replace your personal communications. You can't develop trust electronically.

Communication with Your Boss

In addition to effectively communicating with your followers, another person you must maintain effective communication with is your boss. Whether your boss is great or your relationship is strained, it is your responsibility to facilitate productive communications. Few successful people have worked for excellent bosses all of their career. In fact, the survey referenced in Chapter One found that only 14 percent of leaders are a positive role model for their followers. Somewhere along the way, most are faced with dealing with bosses who do not share their values, and the relationships are not positive. Jesus taught us how to deal with an arrogant boss in the parable of the persistent widow in Luke 18. In that parable, her "boss" neither feared God nor cared about the people. This combination could lead to an unhealthy environment, wouldn't you say? Jesus' direction was simple: *"Always pray and do not give up."*[14] Even when you choose to no longer work for a person, never give up your prayers for him.

Upward communication goes against organizational gravity and requires discipline and courage. *If you make communication a priority with your boss, your relationship will improve, and you will achieve better results.* Here are three tips for effective upward communication:

- *Be Accurate and Complete.* Delivering partial or inaccurate information is worse than delivering no information at all. The boss does not have time to fill in blanks, guess about what you really mean, or chase you down to get the real facts. Decisions will be made with wrong assumptions if you have not provided accurate and complete information.

- *Be on Time.* One of the principal elements in evaluating candidates for promotion is the dependability of a person to deliver information on time without surprises. Avoid surprises at all costs. People can react to what they know and recovery can be made. Surprises have a tendency to make you and your boss look bad. Communicate facts quickly and accurately to avoid an uncomfortable surprise which creates an emotional reaction that seldom leads to positive results. Be on time, be consistent, and avoid surprises.

- *Keep It Simple and Concise.* Actions will be taken when you are not there. Make sure your communication is simple, to the point, and understandable. The Lord's Prayer is only 56 words. It doesn't take a lot of words to make a point and to make a difference.

BOSS COMMUNICATION REQUIREMENTS

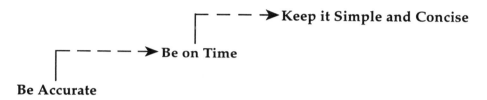

A positive, productive working relationship with your boss is important for your job satisfaction. To nurture that relationship and have a better understanding of your boss, be able to answer these questions:

- What are the goals of your boss?
- What does your boss expect from you in performance, communication, and feedback?
- In what areas does your boss feel uncomfortable, and how can you help?
- What can you do to make your boss look good?

The time you spend developing a positive relationship with your boss will yield improved performance and increased job satisfaction for both you and the boss.

Communication with Your Heavenly Father

Your most important communication is with your heavenly Father. Prayer is our personal, intimate communication with God. When that communication with God breaks down, we are subjected to making decisions we do not want to make. *To be a follower of Jesus, prayer is essential to our happiness and success.*

Make the time to pray. The Bible provides explicit direction in our communication with our heavenly Father:

- Create dedicated time to pray, time when you can pray and listen to God's direction. Prayer is two-way communication between you and God. Take the time to listen to God's direction for you. *"Be still and know that I am God."*[15]

- Pray with an open Bible. Our direction from God comes from an intimate prayer life and our study of the Word. The Bible says, *"In quietness and trust is your strength."*[16] Our quietness comes from our prayers, and our trust comes from our eternal hope in God's word.

- Pray whenever and wherever. The Bible says, *"Do not put out the Spirit's fire."*[17] The way to keep the fire burning is through an ongoing prayer life. You quench the fire by not praying, not studying the Bible, and not giving thanks to God!

- Be specific in your prayers. When the blind beggar asked Jesus to have mercy on him, Jesus asked him, *"What do you want me to do for you?"* Jesus knew what the man desired, but only after he specifically said *"Lord, I want to see"*[18] did Jesus restore his sight. Be specific in your requests.

Any day without spending time with the Father is a wasted day. If you are uncomfortable praying, pray more. There are no instant prayer warriors; you learn to pray by praying.

Communicating with Your Heavenly Father

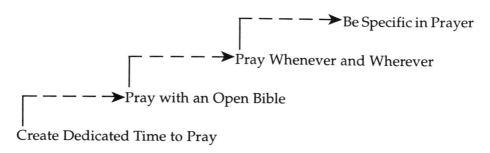

Be Specific in Prayer

Pray Whenever and Wherever

Pray with an Open Bible

Create Dedicated Time to Pray

Summary

Effective communication is critical to your success as a leader. Your ability to connect with people from different backgrounds and experiences is a talent that has to be learned and nurtured in your daily leadership activities. Here are some suggestions:

- Be creative in your communication.
- Have a specific plan to communicate with your followers and your boss.
- Focus on your critical success factors.
- Be in personal contact with your followers.
- Develop trust through your communication.
- Make communication with your heavenly Father your top priority.

Your highest form of communication is your example. People hear what you say and how you say it, but people respond to what they see you do. Be aware of the messages your actions are communicating!

It is up to you to decide how to speak to your people. Make people who work for you feel important. If you honor and serve them, they'll honor and serve you.

—Mary Kay Ash

OFFICE PRAYER

Lord Jesus, as I enter this work place, I bring your presence with me;
I speak Your peace, Your grace, and
Your perfect order into the atmosphere of this office;
I acknowledge your Lordship over all that I will speak,
think, decide, and accomplish within these walls.

Lord Jesus, I thank You for the gifts You have deposited in me;
I do not take them lightly,
but commit to using them responsibly and well.
Give me a fresh supply of truth and
beauty on which to draw as I do my job;

Anoint my creativity, my ideas, and my energy so that even the
smallest task may bring You honor.

Lord, when I am confused, guide me;
When I am weary, energize me;
Lord, when I am burned out,
infuse me with the light of your Holy Spirit.
May the work that I do and the way I do it bring hope, life, and
courage to all that I come in contact with today;
And, oh Lord, even in this day's most stressful moments ...
may I rest in You.
In Your strong name I pray, Lord Jesus, Amen.

Author Unknown

CHAPTER SEVEN

CONFLICT RESOLUTION

Consider it pure joy, my brothers, whenever you face trials of many kinds, because you know that the testing of your faith develops perseverance.

— *James 1:2-3*

THE PRINCIPLE OF CONFLICT RESOLUTION

Leadership results improve to the extent that the leader is able to timely remove the obstacles inhibiting his or her followers.

An effective leader is results-oriented and accepts the responsibility to ensure that conflicts are resolved. Conflicts within work groups can be devastating to the mission and to the team members unless they are addressed quickly and fairly. Great leaders are aware of what is happening within their teams and are seldom blind-sided by major problems. The Bible says, *"A sensible man watches for problems ahead and prepares to meet them. The simpleton never looks, and suffers the consequences."*[1] The successful leader has the ability to immediately recognize a problem and has the courage to address the problem before it becomes an emergency.

The Bible provides explicit direction concerning conflicts. Moses was faced with a problem that most leaders face somewhere along the way. In Exodus 17:4 he cries to the Lord, *"What am I to do with these people? They are almost ready to stone me."* We all can relate to that. Things might not be going as planned; our people are unhappy and may be ready to revolt. The Lord directed Moses to stay ahead (focused), take some helpers, and go.[1] Just when the followers were at the point of revolting, God provided for Moses.

Nehemiah was a great leader and problem-solver. Recognizing that God had chosen him to lead the Jews to rebuild Jerusalem's walls, he took charge and led a team to solve the problem. Nehemiah used his talents of vision, organization, encouragement, and communication to get the walls built. He took swift action to solve the situation and follow God's direction.[2]

Jesus taught about conflicts that could be a test of our faith. In the midst of a storm, when Jesus was asleep in the boat with his disciples, the disciples panicked, saying, *"We are going to drown."* They asked their leader, *"Don't you care?"*[3] They imagined the worst and lost their faith in the power of the one with them. Jesus said, *"Why are you still afraid? Do you still have no faith?"* Even after all the miracles they had seen Jesus perform, they still were not sure he could solve *their* problem. He corrected the situation and moved on.

In Proverbs, we learn the first conflict resolution process. First, get the facts: *"He who answers without listening—that is his folly and his shame."* Second, try new things: *"The heart of the discerning acquires knowledge, the ears of the wise seek it out."* Third, listen to both sides of the issue: *"The first to present his case seems right, till another comes forward and questions him."*[4]

Cain and Abel were the first examples of conflict within our families.[5] Due to his anger, Cain made bad choices based on emotions out of control. Problems can never be solved effectively while you are angry. You are guaranteed to make bad choices with permanent consequences, setting the stage for additional bad choices.

Most leaders do not enjoy solving problems. Effective problem-solving is hard work, and it is human nature to dislike conflicts. By definition, problems mean that something is not right, and unless the situation is personally affecting them, most people would rather do anything than attack the problem. But if the problem is affecting them, they want it fixed immediately!

The Leader's Problem-Solving Role

A leader has no alternative but to address conflicts that the followers are not able to solve. People will always have conflicts, and the leader will always be needed to help solve them. Your first challenge, as a leader, is to look at the situation positively and to recognize that your value is in discovering acceptable solutions. One of the leader's responsibilities is to sacrifice time and energy to objectively deal with the problems of others. Norman Vincent Peale said, "Positive thinking is how you think about a problem. Enthusiasm is how you feel about a problem. The two together determine what you do about a problem." The successful problem-solver must be positive and enthusiastic while searching to find workable solutions.

The role of the leader is to create an atmosphere in which followers can deal with their own issues and to facilitate the process of solving problems. Such as the following:

- Computers continually breaking down, leading to employee frustration and decreasing productivity
- Barriers that are keeping your people from completing their task
- Issues that prevent your work group's progress
- Not having the appropriate tools to complete tasks

It is the leader's responsibility to address all of these issues. However, surveys have indicated that more than 80 percent of problems encountered by corporate leadership involve interpersonal conflicts within the work group. The Bible says, *"If a house is divided against itself that house cannot stand."*[6] These conflicts cannot be neglected on the premise that they will work themselves out—they won't. The longer problems are allowed to continue, the more likely they are to spread through the work group and ultimately throughout the company. When a conflict continues, more people are affected, and the cost to solve the problem escalates dramatically.

Solve the Problem Now!

The 1-10-100 rule of problem-solving illustrates the impact of allowing an issue to persist. This rule states that a conflict solved quickly and efficiently between two people can be solved with the equivalent of one unit of time, money, or resources. That same problem, if it is not addressed at the source but is allowed to spread into a work group, will then require the equivalent of ten units of time, money, or resources to solve. More emotions and perceptions now must be addressed because the problem has spread.

If the problem continues to exist and is allowed to work through the company or to customers, it will then require the equivalent of at least one hundred units of measurement to solve. That is one hundred times what it would have cost to solve the same problem in the beginning. I am sure you have seen minor situations become major catastrophes because the problem was not addressed timely and efficiently. Solve problems before they become an emergency!

Impact of the Timing of Solving Problems

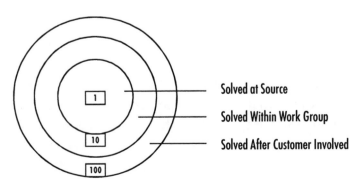

Solved at Source

Solved Within Work Group

Solved After Customer Involved

Get the Facts

The key to conflict resolution is understanding what the problem really is. Most conflicts are 70 percent **perception-based** and 30 percent **fact-based**. We have all seen two people in furious disagreement over what they think the other one is thinking. The leader's role is to decrease the emotions caused by false perceptions and increase the energy focused on the facts. The Bible says, *"Get the facts at any price, and hold on tightly to all the good sense you can get."*[7] Sometimes it requires all your energy just to hold on tightly to your good sense while you are getting the facts. This illustration is a story told by a college professor about a letter from his student to her parents:[8]

Dear Mother and Dad,

Since I left for college I have been remiss in writing to you. I am really sorry for my thoughtlessness in not writing before. I will bring you up to date now, but before you read on, please sit down. You are not to read any further unless you are sitting down. Okay?

Well, then, I am getting along pretty well now. The skull fracture I got when I jumped out of the window of my dormitory when it caught fire shortly after my arrival here is pretty well healed. I spent only two weeks in the hospital, and now I can see almost normally and get those sick headaches only once a day.

Fortunately, the fire in the dormitory (and my jump) was witnessed by an attendant at the gas station near the dorm, and he was the one who called the fire department and the ambulance. He also visited me in the hospital, and since I had nowhere to live because of the burnt-out dormitory, he was kind enough to invite me to share his apartment with him. It's really just a basement room, but it's kind of cute.

He is a fine boy, and we have fallen deeply in love and are planning to get married. We haven't set the exact date yet, but it will be before my pregnancy begins to show. Yes, Mother and Dad, I am pregnant. I know how much you are looking forward to being grandparents, and I know you will welcome the baby and give it the same love and devotion and tender care you gave me when I was a child.

The reason for the delay in our marriage is that my boyfriend has a minor infection, which prevents us from passing our premarital blood tests, and I carelessly caught it from him. But I know that you will welcome him into our family with open arms. He is kind and, although not well educated, he is ambitious. Although he is of a different race and religion from ours, I know your often-expressed tolerance will not permit you to be bothered by that.

Now that I have brought you up to date, I want to tell you that there was no dormitory fire. I did not have a skull fracture. I was not in the hospital. I am not pregnant. I am not engaged. I am not infected, and there is no boyfriend in my life. However, I am getting a D in History and an F in Biology, and I wanted you to see these grades in their proper perspectives.

Your loving daughter,

Susie

Remember, hold on tightly to all good sense while you are getting the facts! The leader's responsibility is to properly identify the facts, decrease incorrect perceptions, and offer solutions to the problem. Most interpersonal problems in any organization develop because the leader has failed to grasp the true nature of the problem and is not focused on solving the right problem.

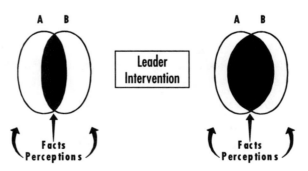

Personal Conflicts with Followers

When you are personally involved in a conflict with a follower, it is best to put time between the situation and your response instead of trying to solve the problem immediately. Since you cannot take back what you say, and most people do not say the right thing when they are emotionally involved, it is best not to speak until you have time to consider the consequences of your words.

Every leader will be faced with responding to a personal conflict between himself and a follower. No one is immune to this uncomfortable position; however, few will be faced with a situation as challenging as the one that a well-known leader had to address. Try to mentally put yourself in this position. You and your management team leave town for a leadership retreat. After spending a few days at the retreat, you return to find your business destroyed by fire and every asset of your company lost. Then you discover that your family and employees are missing. You wouldn't think it could get much worse, but it does. Your management team turns on you and blames you for the loss. Wouldn't it be easy to be bitter, hurt, and cynical? Imagine how you would feel about the situation, your management team, and your leadership role.

The conflict that David experienced with his warriors was even more tragic than the scenario you just read. While David and his men were away to fight a battle, the enemy attacked and burned their village. The enemy also took captive the soldiers' wives, sons, and daughters. Imagine a scene so horrible that these strong warriors *"wept aloud until they had no strength left to weep."* The men blamed their leader, David, for their tragic loss and talked of stoning him. You can feel for David. He was hurting because his family had also been captured, and now his own soldiers had turned on him. Even in this tragic situation, David did not panic or fight with his soldiers. He kept his cool and put some time and space between the conflict and his response. He left to seek a quiet place to sort through the issues, and he *"found strength in the Lord his God."* During his time of prayer, peace, and solitude, he was able to find a course of action that led to a solution.[9]

There is much wisdom to the practice of "sleeping on a problem" when you are personally involved in the situation. Follow David's example the next time you are faced with a personal conflict with a follower. Keep your cool, don't panic or fight, go to a quiet place, and seek God's direction for solutions to your problem.

Whatever you do, never respond in anger. Does anything good happen when you are angry? No. Your ability to reason is diminished, and the chances are that you will harm your relationship with others. Anger is a direct violation of God's commandment to love. An angry response will risk two of your most important personal possessions, your Christian witness and integrity. Follow the Bible's guidance in James 1:19-20: *"Everyone should be quick to listen, slow to speak and slow to become angry. For man's anger does not bring about the righteous life that God desires."* Keep your cool!

Problem-Solving Process

For problems that are not interpersonal conflicts, successful problem-solving requires following a defined process. In the 1800s Vilfredo Pareto, an Italian economist, discovered that about 20 percent of the families in Italy controlled about 80 percent of the wealth. Discovering that this uneven distribution applied in many other situations as well, Pareto formulated what has become known as the Pareto Principle, or the 80/20 Rule. That rule states that most results (80 percent) are produced by a small number of causes (20 percent). The successful leaders spend their time identifying the few problems that contribute to the major productivity barriers and then follow a process to solve those problems.

An effective problem-solving process involves four steps:

STEP 1   *Define the problem in writing.* Stating the problem on paper clarifies the situation. Answer the following questions:

What is the current situation?

What is the impact?

What is the desired state of affairs?

Everyone has to agree on the answers to these three questions before you can move to the next step. Once you complete this step, your problem is well on the way to being solved.

STEP 2   *Analyze potential solutions.* What are the alternatives, and are they doable? Gather the information required to make a decision:

Decide what you need to know.

Collect the necessary data.

Determine the most influential factors.

You will know you have completed this step when you understand the current extent of the problem and know enough about the problem to solve all or part of it for good.

STEP 3   *Develop the promising solutions.* Now that the data is available, you can make an educated decision about which direction to pursue.

Identify the best solution to solve the problem.

Develop an implementation plan.

STEP 4   *Execute the plan.*

Gain commitment from affected parties.

Communicate the plan.

Monitor the results.

This is the easiest step to problem-solving if the other three steps have been done properly.

Systematic Problem-Solving

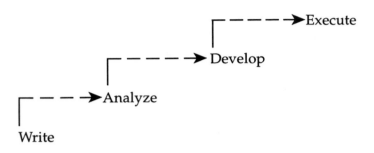

A creative, fun, and effective problem-solving technique you can use as a team-building exercise or when all solutions have been exhausted is called the contingency diagram. This technique allows your team to look at ways to make the problem worse and then create a preventive plan to ensure that the worst does not happen. Many times, people are more creative in figuring out ways to make things worse rather than better. For example, if you are looking for ways to ensure your success, the contingency diagram would force you to look for ways to ensure failure and then you can create a plan to prevent failure from happening. You would brainstorm with your work group and explore how to make sure failure occurs. What can we do that will provide us no chance to succeed? Your brainstorm session may yield results similar to this:

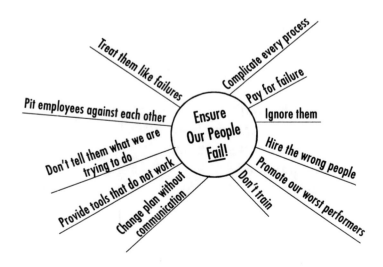

Then, once you have exhausted all of the ways to make the problem worse, develop a plan to ensure that none of the actions that will ensure failure have an opportunity to happen.

Actions to Prevent Each of These from Happening
—
—
—
—
—
—

This technique will generate ideas that might be hard to generate with a conventional problem-solving approach. The contingency diagram is fun, involves the team in developing alternatives, and creates ownership for the agreed-upon actions. Try it.

Summary

It is the leader's role to clear a path to success by resolving conflicts. It is important to solve problems quickly, based on facts, and to have a systematic process to solve the problems. Listen passionately, ask questions, agree on the decision, and move forward. When you are personally involved in the conflict, allow some time between the conflict and your response, and seek God's guidance.

> *The significant problems we face cannot be solved at the same level of thinking we were when we created them.*
> —*Albert Einstein*

How Successful Leaders Carry the Cross

Louis Kruger
Sales Manager
Jostens

My job dictates that I spend a lot of time with young people—primarily high school juniors and seniors. Sometimes the students are a test of my patience and attitude, but a great opportunity to witness. The primary way I carry my cross at the schools is to let them see Jesus through my positive attitude. Many times they ask how I can stay positive, which opens the door for me to witness. The way I am able to stay positive is to have my spiritual life right. If I slack off my prayer and study time, Satan wears on me, and his influence is reflected in my attitude.

I am also aware of the effect of procrastinating when God provides opportunities. Satan tells me to not worry because I have plenty of time to witness and I'll be able to do it later. Carrying my cross is making a choice not to procrastinate in doing God's work. Procrastination will kill your Christian walk.

Another way I witness is to encourage students who have the courage to wear a Christian T-shirt or What Would Jesus Do bracelet. I build them up through positive reinforcement.

In many situations the only thing we have control over is our attitude, so I choose to have a positive one every day. I normally have only one opportunity to leave a positive impression on the students. I try to make the best of that opportunity.

CHAPTER EIGHT

OPTIMISM

Whatever things are true, whatsoever things are honest, whatsoever things are just, whatsoever things are pure, whatsoever things are lovely, whatsoever things are of good report, if there be any virtue, and if there be any praise, think on these things.

— Philippians 4:8 (KJV)

THE PRINCIPLE OF OPTIMISM

Leadership results improve in direct proportion to the self-concept and optimism of the leader.

Optimism is not the result of living in a Pollyanna world where bad things do not happen to good people. Optimism is the result of a person's desire and effort to accept a difficult situation and make that situation the best possible. All leaders are faced with setbacks and unexplainable events that could be devastating. People and situations change, and our faith is tested through fear of the unknown. The optimistic leader believes that defeat is a temporary setback isolated to a given situation. He expects the best possible outcome and concentrates on the most hopeful aspects of what might appear to be a hopeless situation. The optimistic leader understands that what you expect does influence what happens.

Optimism increases energy and allows you and your people to focus on long-term goals. The effective leader chooses to remain optimistic and search for the best, even in times of stress and uncertainty. They refuse to waste their energy fretting about situations over which they have no control. The great leaders approach every difficulty with optimism and determination.

Combat the Enemies

The two greatest enemies of optimism are worry and negative emotions. Worry creates fear, drains your energy, prevents you from achieving your potential, and obstructs your followers from obtaining their goals. Not much good can happen when you are paralyzed with worry.

Once there was a study that asked people what they worried about over a period of time and tracked what happened to those worries. These were results:

- Forty percent of the worries concerned things that never happened.
- Thirty percent of the worries concerned things in the past, and nothing could be done about them.
- Twelve percent were needless worries about health.
- Ten percent were petty worries about unimportant things.
- Only eight percent of the worries concerned anything substantial.

Only half of the eight percent involved things that could be changed and were in their control. According to this study, then ninety-six percent of what we worry is beyond our control to change. What we do control is our action to keep the worry from happening. *The antidote to worry is to make the decision to take action to prevent the worry from happening.*

Jesus was explicit in his teachings about worry. In the Sermon on the Mount[1] He asked, *"Who of you by worrying can add a single hour to his life?"* Later He said, *"I tell you, do not worry about your life."* Jesus knew the negative effects of worry. It damages your health, it consumes your thoughts, and it paralyzes your decision-making process. A leader consumed by worry cannot effectively lead at home, church, or the office. Paul taught us not to worry about anything, but to pray about everything: *"Do not be anxious about anything, but in everything, by prayer and petition, with thanksgiving, present your request to God."*[2] To worry less, you need to pray more.

In the parable of the four soils, Jesus taught about those that hear the word of God but *"as they go their way become choked by life's worries, riches, and pleasures and they do not mature."*[3] Worry indicates a lack of faith and consumes the energy and optimism that are ours through God.

Jesus taught, *"So do not worry, saying, 'What shall we eat?' or 'What shall we drink?' or 'What shall we wear?' For the pagans run after all these things, and your heavenly Father knows that you need them."* Leaders today weight themselves down with the same worries. We worry about what we will eat and drink, about the clothes we will wear, and about tomorrow. God's promise is that if we *"seek first his kingdom and his righteousness, all these things shall be given to us."*[4]

Surely no one told you that leadership would be easy! Leading people is a struggle! All followers have different personalities and are motivated differently. They have personal problems, financial issues, concerns about children, and plenty of other distractions. While you are leading others, you still have your own personal problems! Jesus acknowledged that we do struggle with our responsibilities, and He provided for our relief. *"Come to me, all you who are weary and burdened, and I will give you rest. Take my yoke upon you and learn from me, for I am gentle and humble in heart, and you will find rest for your souls. For my yoke is easy and my burden is light."*[5] Notice that He did not promise us a life without burdens, but He did provide a way to handle the burdens we carry.

To combat worry, follow these steps:

- Get the facts—Most worry is based on false assumptions. Get the real facts, and don't let yourself worry about the many other things that drain your energy.
- Consider the worst possible outcome—If this worry is among the four percent over which you have control, what will be the effect if it does come to pass? Once you discover the worst possible outcome, you will often find that it is not as bad as you thought. Your stress comes from not understanding the worst possible outcome, so you can deal with it.
- Begin to improve on the worst possible outcome—Create a plan that will begin purposeful action to ensure that the worst does not happen. It is difficult to worry about things you are working to improve. Again, the antidote to worry is taking action to prevent something from happening.
- Pray about it and let it go—If you have done everything you can to prevent the worry from happening, and you have asked for God's help, let it go. Your worrying is not helping anyone or anything. In fact, it is probably making you and those around you miserable.

What About Those Negative Emotions?

The second enemy of optimism is negative emotions. Everyone has negative emotions and must create a way to minimize the damage they can cause. Negative emotions tend to show up at the worst time and cause us to do and say things we regret. Emotions such as hate, fear, doubt, jealousy, self-pity, anger, and resentment will never add to your leadership success. To combat negative emotions, try these six steps:

- Face the reality of the negative emotion—What you are experiencing is real. You are feeling its effects and it is having a negative impact on your leadership. Don't deny it; do something about it.
- Do not criticize yourself—you are human. Beating yourself up for expressing human emotions creates more negativity and does nothing to solve the problem or make you a more effective leader.

- Do not blame anyone—Placing the blame will not solve the problem. Avoid blaming anyone for anything. Blame always focuses on the past and does not do anything to solve your current problem.
- Accept responsibility—The faster you can learn to say, "I am responsible for my negative emotion of _____," the more quickly you can be productive again. Responsibility always focuses on the future and is the beginning of turning the negative emotion into a positive action.
- Ask for forgiveness—If you have any unfinished business contributing to the negative feelings, go to the person and ask him or her to forgive you. This action will release the guilt, anger, jealousy, etc., from you and allow you to go forward.
- Pray about it—Ask for God's forgiveness, accept His forgiveness, and be the positive, optimistic leader He wants you to be.

Remember Who Is in Control

In times when you and your people are struggling, the way for the Christian leader to be optimistic is to *accept that God is in control.* I know! When my business was struggling to get off the ground and it seemed hopeless, I came home to my wife, Karen, and was having myself a real pity party. Karen would have none of it—she said that it had been obvious that God had provided in the past, and she knew that He would continue to provide. She said that I could not quit if I wanted to—"you can only quit what you control, and God has control of our business." She was right. Nothing in God's control is out of control. It was my job to use the talents I had been given to follow God's direction. *It is difficult to worry while you are energetically working toward a plan!* That realization became a turning point in changing my worry to optimism and accepting whatever the Lord provides.

Don't Give Up

When the pressures of leadership make a situation look hopeless, remember that perseverance is the principal difference between success and failure. To keep your situation in perspective, consider the pressures this man must have endured:

> Failed in business in '31
> Defeated for the Legislature in '32
> Failed in business again in '34
> Sweetheart died in '35
> Had a nervous breakdown in '36
> Defeated in election in '38
> Defeated for Congress in '43
> Defeated for Congress in '46
> Defeated for Congress in '48
> Defeated for Congress in '55
> Defeated for Vice President in '56
> Defeated for Senate in '58
> Elected President in '60

> This man was Abraham Lincoln.

A major difference between successful leaders and leaders that do not achieve the desired results is that successful leaders insist on reliving past success. They find ways to duplicate their success, even though the situation has changed. The unsuccessful insist on reliving their past failures and wind up duplicating those failures. Make sure you keep an optimistic outlook about the future by learning from the past.

Positive People Produce Positive Results

Another key to keeping an optimistic outlook is to *surround yourself with positive people* who will work with you to figure out ways to work through trials. Allowing negative people in your work group will destroy your morale and your followers' morale faster than any action of a competitor. One negative person has the ability to influence hundreds of others. For whatever reason, the negative person has a far greater influence than the positive person. The Bible cautions us about surrounding ourselves with the wrong crowd. Proverbs states, *"Do not make friends with a hot tempered man, do not associate with one easily angered, or you may learn his ways and get yourself ensnared."*[6] Paul wrote, *"Do not be misled: bad company corrupts good character."*[7] You cannot afford to have negative people on your team. Negative people drain your energy, destroy your confidence, and slash your productivity. You've seen it. When a different idea is developed and everyone is excited, they deflate the balloon by saying, "Yeah, but ... " and proceed to tell you why the idea won't work. Thanks a lot! There are plenty of people who can give you the "yeah, buts." Let them work for your competitors. Surround yourself with the ones that will tell you, "Yeah, and here's how we can do it!"

We are by nature protective and concerned about our children's chosen friends. Rightly so. We know that one of the most important decisions our kids make is choosing the right people to hang around with. Because of their value-based friendship, they build each other up and keep each other out of trouble. Choosing friends with conflicting values will lead to some very difficult choices that we don't want our children to make. We want them to associate with energetic, positive people. Your work group is the same. Choose positive people who have the same values and share your commitment to the mission. *The more you enjoy the people at work, the more you will enjoy your work.* Positive people will create energy and help you figure out ways to succeed. According to EPC International, strategic stress consultants, the number-one key to managing executive stress is to *surround yourself with positive people.*[8] Associating with positive people will make your job more rewarding and life much easier!

Look for the Best

Maintaining an optimistic outlook requires you to *always look for the best in yourself and others.* Many times, being positive goes against our human nature. We are the most critical of ourselves. People are far more careful of what they say to others than what they say to themselves. It has been said that 95 percent of our inner-self talk is negative—"I can't, I won't, we don't, no one," etc. Should we feel that way about ourselves? Certainly not. You are not inferior to anyone. The faster you accept the fact that you are okay, the sooner you will be able to enjoy your leadership role.

Even when you are stressed to the max, maintain a positive attitude by being a champion at positive self-talk that replaces negative thoughts. Replace "I can't" with "I can"; "I won't" with "I will"; "we don't" with "we do"; and "no one" with "we are the ones." It will make a difference in how you feel about yourself and in your ability to be an effective leader.

How we choose to react to a situation determines our happiness. G. W. Target, in his essay "The Window," tells the story of two men confined to hospital beds in the same room. Both were seriously ill and were not allowed much diversion—no television, radio, or books. Their friendship developed over months of conversation. They discussed every possible subject in which they both had interest or experience, from family to jobs to vacations, as well as much of their own personal histories.

Neither man left his bed, but one was fortunate enough to be next to the window. As part of his treatment he could sit up in bed for just one hour a day. At this time he would describe the world outside to his roommate. In very descriptive terms he would bring the outside world inside to this friend, describing to him the beautiful park he could see, with its lake and the many interesting people he saw spending their time there. His friend began to live for those descriptions.

After a particularly fascinating report, the one man began to think it was not fair that his friend got to see everything while he could see nothing. He was ashamed of his thoughts, but he had quite a bit of time to think, and he couldn't get this out of his mind. Eventually his thoughts began to take their effect on his health, and he became even more ill, with a disposition to match.

One evening his friend, who sometimes had difficulty breathing, awoke with a fit of coughing and choking and was unable to push the button for the nurse to come to his aid. The frustrated, sour man lay there looking at the ceiling, listening to the struggle for life next to him, and doing nothing.

The next morning the day nurse came in to find the man by the window dead.

After a proper interval, the man who was so eager to see out the window asked if he could be moved, and his wish was quickly granted. As soon as the room was empty, the man struggled up on his elbow to look out the window and fill his spirit with the sights of the outside world.

It was then he discovered that the window faced a blank wall.[9]

Our happiness and ability to remain optimistic will never be achieved by obtaining what we perceive others to have. We control our outlook based on our ability to be thankful for our own situation ... whatever it might be.

Maintaining an Optimistic Outlook

In the December 1996 *Golf Magazine*, Tom Kite, a successful golfer and the 1997 U.S. Ryder Cup captain, gave some great advice on keeping an optimistic outlook. His advice is a direct parallel to the guidance that Paul gave us in his writings.

Kite: Don't dwell on your mistakes. Keep your chin up and look to the next shot.

Paul: *"Forgetting what is behind and straining toward what is ahead, I press heavenward in Christ Jesus."* Philippians 3:13-14

Kite: Think positive. Focus your attention on hitting great shots and on enjoying the game you love.

Paul: *"I can do everything through Him that gives me strength."* Philippians 4:13

Kite: Throw away fear. Trust your instincts. Play to play great with a mind free from fear and doubt.

Paul: *"For God does not give us a spirit of timidity, but a spirit of power, of love, and of self discipline."* 2 Timothy 1:7

Kite: Keep the dream alive. Don't abandon your aspirations.

Paul: *"I want to know Christ, and the power of his resurrection and the fellowship of sharing in his sufferings, becoming like him in his death."* Philippians 3:10

Summary

A pessimistic leader always brings disaster. Consistent, positive results are achieved only through consistent, positive leadership. Stay focused on your goals while searching for the few ways to achieve them, and don't worry about the many ways that may not work.

If you are a Christian, your eternal worries are over! You are one of the few people on earth who know, without a doubt that their future is secure. Enjoy the trials and depend on God to meet your needs—that is how to remain optimistic regardless of what is going on around you.

Four Keys to Being an Optimistic Leader

1. Combat the enemies—worry and negative emotions.
2. Accept that God is in control!
3. Surround yourself with positive people.
4. Always look for the best in yourself and others.

Things turn out best for the people who make the best of the way things turn out.

—*John Wooden*

ATTITUDE

The longer I live, the more I realize the impact of attitude on life.

Attitude, to me, is more important than facts.

It is more important than the past, than education, than money, than circumstances, than failures, than successes, than what other people think or say or do.

It is more important than appearances, giftedness or skill.

It will make or break a company . . . a church . . . a home . . . a relationship.

The remarkable thing is WE HAVE A CHOICE everyday regarding the attitude we embrace for the day.

We cannot change the past . . .

We cannot change the fact that people will act in a certain way.

We cannot change the inevitable.

The only thing we can do is play on the one string we have, and that is attitude.

I am convinced that life is 10% what happens to me, and 90% how I react to it.

— Charles Swindoll

CHAPTER NINE

POSITIVE CHANGE MANAGEMENT

So they shook their feet in protest against them and went to Iconium.
And the disciples were filled with joy and with the Holy Spirit.

— *Acts 13:51-52*

THE PRINCIPLE OF POSITIVE CHANGE MANAGEMENT

Leadership results improve to the extent that the leader is able to embrace change and accept responsibility for change.

Everyone desires improvement in life, but hardly anyone wants to make change a part of the improvement process. Can we improve without changing something? Does improvement come from just having a desire? Obviously not. Max Dupree might have said it best: "In the end, it is important to remember that we cannot become what we need to be by remaining what we are."[1]

Change involves leaving your comfort zone to try something different. Without change, we all get in a rut of doing the same things the same way. Why are we surprised when we accomplish the same result? A rut can eventually become a grave; the only difference between a rut and a grave is the depth. Improvement is possible only when changes are made to create an opportunity to improve. Change is as natural as breathing, yet many seem to prefer to take their last breath rather than embrace change that can allow things to improve.

The Bible helps us understand the process of changing. Many of the great heroes of the Bible went through major changes in their lives. Most of those changes involved people who some would have thought were unchangeable. The key to their successful change was that they were following God's will. If we are in God's will, change can lead to greater results than could be imagined.

We have already discussed the change that took place in the life of Moses. He resisted and made excuses, yet because the change was God-directed, he became the leader of God's people.[2]

God told Abram, at the age of 75, to take a new direction. Abram obeyed by leaving his country, his people, and his father's household to go to an unknown land. In following God's will, Abram left his security and comfort zone and made a major change even at age 75. He followed God and became the father of the Jewish people.[3]

Jesus changed people *who were willing to be changed.* Through their faith in Jesus, people who were considered unchangeable were changed—lepers, the demon- possessed, and the diseased.

In more recent times, people have created positive change when something happened to redirect them. Levi Strauss was intent on panning for gold when he invented jeans to help the gold diggers. Although he never made it to the gold, he acquired plenty of riches by responding to a need, accepting an unexpected opportunity and creating something positive.

John Pemberton was a pharmacist who experimented with various remedies to heal ailments. He stumbled on a recipe for something that tasted good and was enjoyed by people, even though they were not ailing. That's how Coca-Cola began. John Pemberton took a direction completely different from the one he had planned.

Learning from the Mouse

Several years ago there was an experiment to evaluate reaction to change. Four tubes were laid side by side on the floor. A cube of cheese was placed in the second tube. A mouse was then released, and it immediately went to the first tube. Finding the tube empty, the mouse proceeded to the second tube. There he discovered and ate the cheese, which met his basic need for survival. The mouse then returned to his point of release. The next day the mouse followed the same routine by going to the empty first tube, eating cheese from the second tube, and returning to his point of release. He repeated the same routine for several days.

Finally, realizing that he was wasting time by going to the first tube, the mouse began going directly to the second tube. He ate the cheese, met his need for survival, and went back. This routine also continued for several days.

The people conducting the experiment moved the cheese to the third tube the next day. The mouse went directly to the second tube, where his needs had always been met, and there was no cheese. What do you think was the mouse's response? Did he go back to the first tube looking for the cheese? No. Did he go back to where he started? No. Did he go to the third tube searching for the cheese? No. He chose to stay in the second tube, where his need of survival had always been met, and wait for the cheese to come back to him. If allowed, the mouse would have starved in the tube, waiting for the cheese instead of reacting to the change. Doesn't this sound like the reaction of some people we know? "Let's wait," they say. "We have always done it this way, and it has always worked in the past!"

Two points can be learned from this story. First, if the situation changes—even if your needs have always been met and you are comfortable—react to the change. Things do change and things do improve. The telegraph will never return. Black-and-white televisions will never come back. Manual typewriters are a thing of the past. Plastic record albums are history. Change has not affected just technology. I love some traditions, especially our family traditions. But as my family has grown, we have had to make adjustments to our traditions. I can't worry about the changes; I just have to adapt to the changes. If you are waiting for things to be like they used to be, you could wind up starving like the mouse, or you may be just plain miserable. When situations change, don't sit and wait—always look for your cheese.

The second lesson from the mouse is that while your needs are being met, keep looking for ways to improve. A whole block of cheese could have been in the fourth tube, and the mouse would not have known because he was content having his basic needs met. The time to make improvement is while things are going well and you are successful. The stress level is lower; your decisions are more objective, and you can think more clearly. While things are going well, keep looking for more cheese.

Change is not going away. In fact, there will probably be more changes in technology, thoughts, people, and the economy in the next ten years than there have been in the last hundred years. Be prepared. Your reaction to change and your leadership through change will have a major impact on the success of you and your people.

Why Change Is Resisted

It is a fact that change will be resisted. Even the smallest of changes— like sitting at a different spot at the dinner table—is resisted. People inherently resist change because it is uncomfortable and requires confidence in a new direction and faith in the leader. Regardless of how anyone feels about it, change is necessary for improvement. A wise person once said, "Insanity is doing the same thing you have always done and expecting different results." We have all experienced this kind of insanity at one time or another.

It is important to understand that people will resist change, primarily for four reasons:

1. *The change is out of their control.* They did not create or ask for the change. Any time you feel you are not in control, you become stressed and begin to resist. No one enjoys creating stress by going into the unknown.

    To eliminate the stress, the leader must *earn the follower's trust long before the change occurs.* Change without trust will be fought at every step, and chances for success are few. Your responsibility is to develop trust, preparing for the time when you ask your followers to leave their comfort zone. Leading with integrity, communicating consistent messages, listening to employees' concerns, and treating them with dignity and respect all add deposits in your trust account.

2. *People do not understand why they are changing.* Without understanding why a change is being made, emotions that are tied to the old way cannot be loosened to deal with the facts. People have to know why they are changing before they are willing to let go of the past. Even if they do not agree, change will be accepted more rapidly if everyone knows why the change is occurring.

    By *involving your followers in the alternatives for change,* your chances for successful change improve significantly. Inform them of the options and provide them the opportunity to be involved in analyzing the alternatives and creating the new plan. The more people you involve in analyzing the alternatives, the more ownership of the change your people will have.

    If the change must happen and you control only the delivery of the message, *get support from your informal group leaders* before announcing the change. Ask for their involvement as you deliver the message. Seeking their help builds their confidence and trust in you when the change is announced. Their vocal support can make the difference in the acceptance of the change.

3. *People perceive themselves as unable to change.* Changes in technology have created a fear of change. Some people are not confident they can learn the new technology and are threatened by the change. Change is resisted when people feel they are unable to change. The leader's role is to create confidence in his people and their ability to adjust to the change.

You create confidence by leading your people through the change. Your total commitment and your actions will be what they remember the most. Delivering inconsistent messages will rapidly destroy the trust you have built, and the change will be resisted.

4. *People perceive that the price they have to pay outweighs the reward.* They may think the change is not worth making them uncomfortable. If they do not understand the result or like what they see, they will do anything to make the change fail.

You can help determine the followers enthusiasm of the change by focusing on the result while you are working through the current trials. Did you ever walk into a movie to see the last ten minutes of the show as the hero and heroine head to their life of happiness? All you see is the outcome. But if you watch the movie from the beginning, your perception is completely different, because you know what happens in the end. Your stress level is down, you can relax, and you can enjoy the trials of the movie stars knowing that everything will be okay. As you lead your people through changes, keep focused on the result. Talk about how rewarding the result will be, and enjoy your leadership role through those tough times of change. You do not necessarily have to like the change, but you have to respect it, let go of the past, and move forward.

Change Leads to Improvement

In the January 27, 1997, issue of *Newsweek*, some earlier predictions that turned out to be a little off base were listed. Think of what our lives would be like without the changes that resulted after these predictions.

Everything that can be invented has been invented.
Charles Duell, Commissioner of Patents, 1899

Airplanes are interesting toys, but of no military value.
Marshal Foch, French military strategist, 1911

Television won't be able to hold on to any market it captures after the first six months. People will soon get tired of staring at a plywood box every night.
Darrell Zanuck, Twentieth Century Fox, 1946

I think there is a world market for about five computers.
Thomas J. Watson, IBM, 1943

With over fifteen types of foreign cars already on sale here, the Japanese auto industry isn't likely to carve out a big share of the market for itself.
Business Week, 1968

There is no reason for any individual to have a computer in his home.
Kenneth Olson, founder, Digital Equipment, 1977

Doesn't it sound ridiculous that these leaders could be so shortsighted? Think of all of the fabulous technological advancements that have taken place since these predictions. All of those great inventions were changes and involved leaders who were able to lead others to see end result. The changes we lead our people through today might not have a dramatic effect on the history of mankind, but they can have a positive impact on the lives of your followers.

Summary

Leading people through change is taxing. There is resistance at every point in the process, and the leader has to stay at least one step ahead of the resisters. Keep this Scripture in mind: *"Let us not become weary of doing good, for at the proper time we will reap a harvest if we do not give up."*[4] Change is here to stay. The philosopher Heraclitus is credited with having said, "The only constant is change." He probably heard that statement from his ancestors, and he lived in the fifth century BC! Embrace change, because when you stop changing, you stop improving.

Before leading your people through their next change, ask yourself the following questions:

Positive Change Management Checklist	**Yes**	**No**
1. Is the change worthwhile?	❏	❏
2. Am I prepared to thoroughly communicate the reason for the change?	❏	❏
3. Do my followers trust me enough to work with me through the trials of change?	❏	❏
4. Are my followers capable of making the change?	❏	❏
5. Am I totally committed to the change?	❏	❏
6. Is the timing right for change?	❏	❏
7. Do I expect the change to be successful?	❏	❏
8. Have I prayed about this change?	❏	❏

If the answer to any of these questions is no, your chances for success are not good. Wait until you can honestly answer yes to all of these questions before making the change.

One of the great discoveries a man makes, one of his great surprises, is to find he can do what he was afraid he couldn't do.
—Henry Ford

PRAYER BY AN
UNKNOWN CONFEDERATE SOLDIER

I asked God for strength, that I might achieve.
I was made weak, that I might learn humbly to obey.

I asked for health, that I might do greater things.
I was given infirmity, that I might do better things.

I asked for riches, that I might be happy.
I was given poverty, that I might be wise.

I asked for power, that I might have the praise of men.
I was given weakness, that I might feel the need of God.

I asked for all things, that I might enjoy life.
I was given life, that I might enjoy all things.

I got nothing that I asked for—but everything I had hoped for.
Almost despite myself, my unspoken prayers were answered.

I am among all men most richly blessed.

THE SYNERGY PRINCIPLES CHECKUP

• Communications • Conflict Resolution • Optimism
• Positive Change Management

PERSONAL RATING   1 (low) — 5 (high)

1.   I consistently tell my followers what is required.   _____

2.   I give positive feedback often.   _____

3.   I continually show my followers I care.   _____

4.   I communicate our team's goals and results.   _____

5.   I listen with empathy.   _____

6.   I focus on the few vital activities that lead to success. _____

7.   I communicate effectively with my boss.   _____

8.   I reward what I expect.   _____

9.   I solve relationship problems quickly.   _____

10. I never respond in anger.   _____

11. I surround myself with positive people.   _____

12. I look for the best in myself and others.   _____

13. I look for the cheese.   _____

14. I embrace change.   _____

15. I spend my time in my areas of excellence.   _____

16. I do not worry, because I know God is in control.   _____

Three Areas I Commit to Improve:	My Actions to Improve
1.	1.
2.	2.
3.	3.

INVESTMENT

PRINCIPLES OF
SUCCESSFUL LEADERSHIP

VALUES — SYNERGY

PART THREE

THE INVESTMENT PRINCIPLES

EMPOWERMENT • COURAGE • EXAMPLE • PREPARATION

The moment you choose to make self-development and people development a priority is the moment your leadership results begin to improve dramatically.

CHAPTER TEN

EMPOWERMENT

Give and it shall be given to you; good measure, pressed down, and shaken together, and running over, shall men give into your bosom.
— Luke 6:38 (KJV)

THE PRINCIPLE OF EMPOWERMENT

Leadership results improve as followers are provided the opportunity to accept total ownership of their work.

In *Flight of the Buffalo*,[1] authors James Belasco and Ralph Stayer write of the day they discovered the power of empowering their people: "Then one day I got it. What I really wanted in the organization was a group of responsible, interdependent workers, similar to a flock of geese. I could see the geese flying in their 'V' formation, the leader changing frequently, with different geese taking the lead. I saw every goose being responsible for getting itself to wherever the gaggle was going, changing roles whenever necessary, alternating as a leader, a follower, or a scout. And when the task changed, the geese would be responsible for changing the structure of the group to accommodate, similar to the geese that fly in a 'V' but land in waves. I could see each goose being a leader.

"Then I saw clearly that the biggest obstacle to success was my picture of a loyal herd of buffalo waiting for me, the leader, to tell them what to do. I knew I had to change the pictures to become a different kind of leader, so everyone could become a leader."

Releasing Control

The inherent nature of leaders is to take control and get things done their way. Empowering others to do important tasks sometimes makes leaders uncomfortable and anxious. Regardless of the apprehensions of the leader, excellence can be achieved only through the talents and experience of a team working toward a common goal. No one can achieve excellence by working on his own personal island—excellence is achieved only through the ability to work with others. Principle-based leaders understand that their position provides the opportunity and privilege of training and equipping others to achieve outstanding results. They also recognize that followers must be provided the freedom to learn from their failures as well as their successes. Empowering employees forces leaders to leave our comfort zone, trust others, and release control so that followers can learn and grow.

Jethro's Lessons

Moses discovered that he could not do everything himself. His father-in-law, Jethro, watched him and immediately recognized that Moses was trying to do everything for his people. This is a mistake almost all managers make in their careers. In Exodus 18:17-27, written approximately 3,500 years ago, Jethro teaches us the concept of improved results through empowerment. Jethro's advice is just as applicable today as it was when he mentored Moses:

- *"What you are doing is not good—you will wear yourself out. The work is too heavy for you. You can't do everything by yourself."* Every successful leader comes to the realization that asking others to share the leadership role is best for everybody. The more you involve your followers, the more they are willing to follow.

- *"Listen to me."* Jethro wanted to help. I get the feeling that Jethro had been waiting for the right opportunity to contribute. Most men of wisdom and experience want to share that wisdom but will share only when asked. Successful leaders seek out mentors and leaders and learn from their wisdom.

- *"Be an example to them. Teach them and show them the way to live."* Jethro was advising Moses to provide his people the tools to be successful, to lead them by example, and to teach them what he knew. His direction was for Moses to influence others through his mentoring, training, and example—not doing everything for them.

- *"Select capable men to anoint as officials. Men who fear God are trustworthy and honest."* Jethro was telling Moses to find people he could trust and people who shared the same values. The ability of the men Moses appointed was important, but more important was choosing men of integrity to help lead the people. Qualified people who have the same value system are the people you want helping you lead.

- *"Select capable men from all the people."* Jethro was telling Moses to have diversity in his appointed leaders. The more diversity you have in your work group, the more effectively it will function. Combining the experiences of people with different backgrounds will provide you with better information to make decisions.

- *"Let them bring the difficult cases to you and let them solve the simple cases. This will lighten your load because you share it with your people."* Jethro was directing Moses to spend his time doing what he did best and to allow his people to do the rest.

Jethro predicted that, *"Moses would be able to stand the strain and all your people would go home satisfied."*[2] Not only are delegation and empowerment good for the leader, but they are also good for the followers! Jethro was teaching Moses the positive result of sharing responsibility. His advice is sound: recognize that you need your followers' help, teach them how to help, and surround yourself with God-loving, trustworthy, and honest people. Then empower them to solve their own problems, and intervene only when problems dictate your involvement. This approach lightens your load and provides others a chance to grow! The wisdom of Jethro still rings true. Think of how many mistakes leaders could avoid by listening to the wisdom and experience of our elders. Moses was a wise man; he listened to his mentor and did everything Jethro advised.

Jesus' Example

In his humanity, Jesus knew he alone could not do all that needed to be done. He chose his disciples and empowered them to do what needed to be done. He gave them power and authority, instructing them to *"drive out demons, cure diseases, and preach the kingdom of God."*[3] Jesus told his disciples what they were to do, what to take with them, and how to handle the tough times. They were prepared to do what needed to be done.

Jesus had the power to do whatever he desired. He could have taught through power, but He chose to teach through love. Jesus had power over nature, over spirits, over disease and death,[4] yet He chose to use power only when that power brought about good for others. *His example was to lead others through love, not power.*

Paul empowered Timothy to preach the word. Paul warned Timothy of the trials that were ahead and encouraged him to endure the hardships required to fulfill the mission. After Paul had trained Timothy and the time was right for Timothy to go on his own to spread the word,[5] Paul empowered him with wisdom and experience to preach the gospel.

The Bible illustrates the effective use of teamwork in Romans 12:4: *"Just as each of us has one body with many members, and these members do not all have the same function, so in Christ we who are many form one body, and each member belongs to all the others. We have different gifts, according to the grace given us. If a man's gift is prophesying, let him use it in proportion to his faith. If it is serving, let him serve; if it is teaching, let him teach; if it is encouraging, let him encourage; if it is contributing to the needs of others, let him give generously; if it is leadership, let him govern diligently; if it is to show mercy, let him do it cheerfully."*

Your leadership effectiveness is measured by the results your followers accomplish. If Jesus chose not to do it all by himself, why should we think we can do it all by ourselves? The more effective you are in empowering qualified people, the better results you should expect.

Areas of Excellence

You have areas in which you are the most talented—your areas of excellence. We all have different gifts, and the Bible says, *"Each one should use whatever gift he has received to serve others, faithfully administering God's grace in its various forms."*[6] Whatever talents we have been given we are to use at home, school, and work to glorify God. In your area of excellence, things come easy to you, you enjoy the tasks, and you have a talent with which few people are blessed. To be most effective, you should be spending at least 80 percent of your time working where you are the most productive.

Work where you are the strongest 80 percent of the time

AREAS OF EXCELLENCE

Hire people to supplement your AREAS OF WEAKNESS

Your performance leverage is in surrounding yourself with people with areas of excellence which are different from yours. These are the areas where you are not at your best, areas that drive you crazy and affect your attitude when you are forced to perform those tasks. Allow others who are talented and enjoy working in areas you are weak in take those responsibilities. The best employees are normally those who are working on tasks they have selected in a field they really enjoy. Hire people who sincerely want the freedom to succeed. Empower your trusted associates to do the job by providing them with predetermined guidelines, and hold them accountable for the results. Henry Ford once said, "Coming together is a beginning; keeping together is progress; working together is success." Allowing people the freedom to do their jobs is the key to getting people to work together.

When To Empower

Used correctly, empowerment will improve productivity and morale; however, you are flirting with disaster if you try to empower every decision or every follower. Many situations are not empowerable. In fact, there are at least four areas you should never delegate: hiring your staff, planning the strategy, evaluating direct reports, and recognizing/rewarding performance. When the situation is empowerable, the leader, followers, and situation all dictate the leader's level of involvement. There are two primary leadership styles with many variations, depending upon the situation and the people being led.

Some leaders are task-oriented and communicate the exact duties and responsibilities to be performed. This type of leader answers all of the questions for the follower—what needs to be done, when, where, who is involved, and even how the task is to be accomplished. The methods of accomplishing the task are just as important as the results. This person is very hands-on in his leadership style.

Another style is leading by developing a strong relationship with followers. This style requires mutual trust and allows others to be involved in decisions. The leader is a facilitator of communication, encourages followers to participate in the planning process, and provides the work group autonomy in decision-making. This method of leadership requires a mature leader and mature followers.

Variables of Empowerment

Regardless of which style you are most comfortable with, you have to adjust your leadership style based on the situation and the maturity of your followers. The variables that dictate which style you should lead include the following:

- The importance of the decision—The more important the decision is to the long-term health of the work group, the more involved you need to be. Being uninvolved in a critically important decision is not effective leadership.

- The urgency of the situation—Many times you will not have time to involve others in the decision-making process. You can't be forming committees when there is a blazing fire in the conference room. You have to make a decision and go! If the situation is of extreme urgency, lead with task leadership, even though your normal tendency is relationship leadership.

- Competency of the employee—Does the employee possess the skills and ability to complete the task without management involvement? If not, you are setting the employee up for failure by not being involved.

- The maturity of followers—Have the individuals faced a situation similar to the current task? How did they respond? How mature is their thought process? The less mature work group requires more task-driven leadership. Task leadership is the least effective way to lead. A mature team that has experience in handling the current situation.

- Your confidence in the work group—If you are not confident that your work group can successfully perform a task, establish frequent progress checks along the way. You may lead primarily by relationship but have task checkpoints to ensure that results are being accomplished.

- Confidence of the employee—If employees are not confident that they can successfully complete a task, your intervention is needed to help develop their confidence. Confidence comes from success—help them be successful so they can develop their own confidence. Allowing people to fail because you were so concerned with empowering them destroys the confidence of everyone involved.

Before you automatically empower people, evaluate the situation and your people to avoid empowering their failure. Empowerment is effective only when your people are adequately prepared to handle the situation!

EMPOWERMENT GUIDELINES

LOW ──────────── **LEADER INVOLVEMENT** ──────────── **HIGH**
Relationship-Oriented   Task-Oriented

Not Important	Importance of Decision	Extremely Important
Not Urgent	Urgency of Situation	Extremely Urgent
Inexperienced	Competence of Employee	Very Experienced
Immature	Maturity of Employee	Mature
Low Confidence	Confidence of Employee	Completely Confident
Not Confident	Confidence of Employee	Extremely Confident

Empowerment Parameters

A common mistake some leaders make is empowering their followers without explicitly explaining the parameters. For example, if I empowered my children to develop vacation plans for our family, they would probably make plans for a trip to Europe lasting all summer, with stays in seven countries. If I had not set predetermined guidelines, I would find myself in a position to have to tell them we cannot do what I "empowered" them to develop. Their perception would be that I never really meant to empower them. Because of my failure to explain the guidelines, I would have lost their trust.

The better way to empower them would have been to say, "We have X amount of money to spend, we can stay two weeks, and we need to consider our international flight and time changes." If you are willing to live with any choice they make, then let them make it! If not, add additional guidelines so you can accept their recommendation. *When there is a gap between your perception and your followers' perception of their empowerment, you lose trust.* Set the guidelines; then do everything you can to not change them! Your role is to provide clear direction and allow them the freedom to make the decision.

The Leader's Challenge

One of the greatest challenges for most leaders is to learn how to release control. Many leaders were promoted because they were the best at their previous jobs and were comfortable in the way they did their jobs. As Abraham Maslow put it, "He that is good with a hammer tends to see everything as a nail." When you are leading others, accept the fact that there are always several alternatives to accomplish the same results. In fact, most of the alternatives are ways that you would not choose. Your challenge is to trust the people you have hired to get the results, even when their methods are different from your way. If you have hired the right people for the job and trained them, and if they have the desire to do the job right, let go and give them the control. They will probably achieve results doing it a way that is even better than the way you would have done it.

Empowerment cannot be successful without holding your followers accountable for their results. We are all accountable for our actions. Jesus made his disciples accountable after they were empowered: *"When they returned they reported to Jesus what they had done."*[7] When you empower your people, follow Jesus' example! Train them, give specific instructions, let them know how to react to tough times and give them the freedom to be successful their way.

Leadership: The art of getting someone else to do something you want done because he wants to do it.
—Dwight Eisenhower

Jethro's Eight Steps of Leadership
(Exodus 18:17-27)

1. Recognize that doing everything yourself is not good.

2. Understand your role as leader.

3. Listen to mentors with experience and wisdom.

4. Train your followers to become leaders.

5. Be an example to your people.

6. Select leaders who share your values and are capable of influencing others.

7. Select leaders with different backgrounds and experiences.

8. Intervene only when needed and hold your leaders accountable.

HOW SUCCESSFUL LEADERS CARRY THE CROSS

Mark Shackelford
President and Chief Executive Officer
Kettle Restaurants

I lean on the cross more than I carry the cross. It is difficult for me to talk about a ministry at work. I just try to stay close to God because I have to depend on Him. My goal is to have others see Jesus in me through my honesty and strict adherence to my values.

I spend a lot of time on the road by myself. One of the most impactful decisions of my life was to memorize the Sermon on the Mount during my time on the road. It is amazing how this has given me a different perspective. It has helped me to stay focused on what Jesus taught. I also have offered my kids an incentive to memorize the Sermon on the Mount—I know it will make a great impact on their life.

In work, my best influence is in always treating others the way I want to be treated. I pray for wisdom and guidance daily to keep God in control of my business and personal life.

CHAPTER ELEVEN

COURAGE

And be not conformed to this world; but be ye transformed by the renewing of your mind, that ye may prove what is that good, and acceptable, and perfect, will of God.

— Romans 12:2 (KJV)

THE PRINCIPLE OF COURAGE

Leadership results improve in proportion to the leader's courage to address issues affecting his or her followers.

W hat do you think is the opposite of courage? Many say cowardliness. Others say it is fear. Although both of those answers could apply, I think the most appropriate answer is conformity. Courage is having the guts, nerve, and heart to do things differently and allow progress to develop. Improvement does not happen by taking the road of least resistance and conforming to the way things have always been. That is certainly the easiest route, but conformance does not necessarily require leaders. It takes leadership and courage to lead people through change and maintain focus, even when you have doubts about your own ability.

Courageous Leaders in the Bible

In Gideon's battle with the Midianites,[1] Gideon might have felt secure about going into the battle with 32,000 soldiers. They had prepared, they were ready, and I'm sure they were confident. With 32,000 soldiers, they could overpower the opponent and give themselves credit for a victory. God had other plans. *"Gideon, you have too many men—Israel may think they won with their own strength. Let the ones that want to leave, go."* Twenty-two thousand had no desire to stay. Ten thousand remained. God said, *"There are still too many, take them to the water and I will sift them out for you."* This time only 300 men were left to fight the battle.

Can you imagine how Gideon felt? When he had 32,000 soldiers, 22,000 were afraid, and now he was to go into battle with only 300! Wow! You talk about courage. Gideon had to have complete faith in God. To build Gideon's courage, God allowed Gideon to slip into the enemy camp and overhear a conversation that confirmed that God would deliver the camp to Gideon and his men. God provided the plan, and Gideon had the courage to carry it out against all odds.

Noah had the courage to follow God's plan, even though no one else believed the earth would be covered with water, and everyone thought Noah was crazy to build an ark.[2] The verbal abuse Noah must have taken while he was building the ark must have been discouraging and humiliating. Having the persistence to maintain obedience to God while being taunted, laughed at, and scorned took an incredible amount of courage.

As a youth, David was full of courage and stood up for what he knew was right. He did not view Goliath as a giant, but rather as someone who mocked God, a stance which was not acceptable. David had the courage to trust God. *"The Lord who delivered me from the paw of the lion, and the paw of the bear will deliver me from the hand of this Philistine."*[3] When all of his associates were afraid to take a stand for God, he displayed total trust in God. He had the courage to do what was right, even though his peers discouraged him from trusting God completely.

By standing up for God in front of King Nebuchadnezzar, Shadrach, Meshach, and Abednego showed courage under great pressure. They knew that God would meet their needs, and they chose not to bow down to Nebuchadnezzar's gold or god. They would not sacrifice their values, no matter the price.[4]

Barnabas had the courage to support Saul and let the disciples know that Saul had changed and had become a disciple of Jesus. Barnabas took Saul to the disciples and stood up for him when everyone else was afraid.[5] Without Barnabas' courage, Paul's ministry would have been much more difficult to begin.

Peter and John exhibited courage by standing up for Jesus even under the threat of the Sadducees. Even though they were put in jail, many who heard the message believed, and the number of Jesus' followers grew. Peter and John had the courage to speak the truth.[6]

Paul had the courage to preach for Jesus. After his life radically changed, Paul shared the gospel soon after he had persecuted others for preaching the gospel. After Paul's conversion, people looked at him skeptically, and there was even a conspiracy to kill him. Paul still had the courage to accept his new role and lead thousands to Jesus.[7]

When Jesus was tempted in the desert, He had the courage to stand for what was right, even though he was tempted by his greatest needs. He made a choice that resisted Satan and kept his eyes on the long-range goal. His commitment was undeniable and unwavering.[8]

Courage to Grow

It takes courage to keep making adjustments that lead to your success. The effective leader is not complacent with the way things are, regardless of how great things may appear. He is continually looking for ways to improve and searching for followers that will embrace change so improvements can be made. The Bible says, *"Do not conform to the pattern of the world."*[9] Looking at things differently while improving the situation takes courage, wisdom, confidence, and faith.

It takes courage to accept responsibility and to address issues that are preventing your followers from being on track to accomplish your goals. Blaming mistakes on others does not take courage. In fact, placing blame is a cowardly act. It takes courage to accept the facts without excuse and look to the future with optimism.

It takes courage to tell the truth while providing both positive and negative feedback to your superiors. Telling the truth is not optional for the principle-based Christian leader. Regardless of how the feedback is accepted, it is your responsibility to give the feedback as you perceive it. The most effective way to give negative feedback is to communicate the situation and follow with "Now here is what we can do about it." It removes the tension from both you and your superior. The risk you accept by not giving accurate feedback is far greater than the comfort you might feel in avoiding a conflict.

It takes courage to seek the truth. The higher your leadership position, the more difficult it becomes to get to the truth. Your courage is accepting what the truth really is and leading from that point—not from where you thought you were or where you think you should be. Facing reality is the key to improving a situation. As a leader, you must find the truth and deal with that truth in a positive, forward-thinking manner. If your response to the truth is "shooting the messenger," tight-lipped sarcasm, or denial, why should you expect to hear the truth in the future?

I once heard a story about a man who was elected president of a large company. At his congratulatory party, one of the older employees came to him and asked, "So you are now the president?" "So it seems," the new president replied. The older employee said, "Then you have heard the truth for the last time." Unfortunately, that is the way it is in many organizations. Generate the courage to seek the truth, and accept the truth, and surround yourself with people who will deliver the truth to you.

It takes courage to have faith. The very definition of faith requires courage. Hebrews 11:1 tells us, *"Faith is evidence of things not seen."*

Things not seen? That's the part that makes us uncomfortable. Do you have faith in the abilities of your people? Do you have faith in your product? Do you have faith in God's guidance? If you are in the Word, in prayer, and listening to God's direction, then it is a sin not to have faith in God's direction. It is our responsibility to develop the courage to follow in faith.

It takes courage to reject the cynics. There is no shortage of cynicism in any company or organization. I am sure you can name several cynical people where you work. All organizations have people that sneer, joke about their leaders, and never have the answer to make things better. Some people protect themselves through cynicism. By expecting only the worst in people and things, they will not be disappointed. To be cynical requires no courage or faith. Cynicism doesn't solve issues or help build relationships or do anything but drain energy and emotions. Reject cynics by confronting them with facts, training them, and setting an example with optimism. If the cynics do not change, summon the courage to give them the opportunity to be cynical somewhere else.

It takes courage to speak out for what you believe, even though it might be controversial. The effective leader leaves no doubt as to where he stands. An old saying is, "We are proud to have our freedom to say what we believe anytime and anywhere. We just don't have the courage to do it." Most courageous acts are controversial—that's why they take courage. Stand up for your beliefs, leave no doubt where you stand, and have the courage to be controversial.

It takes courage to persevere. Your courage is ultimately measured by how much it takes to discourage you. Every leader is faced with this decision: *"Do I continue, or is it best to let go of the dream?"* The answer will be made clear only through consistent prayer for direction. If the answer is to stay the course, cling to the promise given in 2 Chronicles 20:17: *"Do not be afraid; do not be discouraged. Go out to face them tomorrow, and the Lord will be with you."* If the answer is to let go of the dream, have the courage to accept God's will for you.

It takes courage to take risks. Risks worth taking are well thought out, are calculated, and lead to an ultimate goal, and the result is worth the risk. Don't be afraid to take a risk. If you do not have some fear, it's not really a risk. The risks that are not worth taking are those that will not deliver the results you need to accomplish your goal, even if you are successful. Theodore Roosevelt spoke of the courage it takes just to accept the risk of failing. "The credit belongs to the man who is actually in the arena; whose face is marred by dust and sweat and blood; who strives valiantly; who errs and comes short again and again; who knows the great enthusiasms, the great devotions, and spends himself in a worthy cause; who at the best knows in the end the triumph of high achievement; and who at the worst, if he fails, at least he fails by daring greatly."

It takes courage to confront problems and responsibilities, especially if we have to admit a mistake or offer an apology. The principal quality that separates us from God is our human ego. The more you depend on God and humble yourself before Him, the easier it is to face issues, admit mistakes, and apologize when wrong.

It takes courage to face criticism. Many leaders are paralyzed by the fear of being criticized. Most people, even strong-willed, self-confident leaders, desire to be liked and popular. The reality is that all leaders must make decisions that may be unpopular and subject to criticism. If you are leading people through change, you cannot expect every one to agree with you or see things your way. You must demonstrate your courage by taking a stand and facing criticism when you are passionate about where you are leading. If you are intent on pleasing everybody, you will never get anything accomplished.

It takes courage to realize that your way might not be the only way to do what you are trying to accomplish. In fact, your way is probably one of hundreds of ways to attain the same goal. Display the courage and confidence to accept the fact that someone else's way might be better, and be willing to try another approach.

Courage to Trust

It takes courage to look beyond the current situation into an area of hope and trust in God to provide for us. In Chuck Swindoll's terrific book, *Hope Again,* he states, "Hope is a wonderful gift from God, a source of strength and courage in the face of life's harshest trials." The following are Dr. Swindoll's examples of God's gift of hope:

- When we are trapped in a tunnel of misery, hope points to the light at the end.
- When we are overworked and exhausted, hope gives us fresh energy.
- When we are discouraged, hope lifts our spirits.
- When we are tempted to quit, hope keeps us going.
- When we lose our way and confusion blurs the destination, hope dulls the edge of panic.
- When we struggle with a crippling disease or a lingering illness, hope helps us persevere beyond the pain.
- When we fear the worst, hope brings reminders that God is still in control.
- When we must endure the consequences of bad decisions, hope fuels our recovery.
- When we find ourselves unemployed, hope tells us we still have a future.
- When we are forced to sit back and wait, hope gives us the patience to trust.
- When we feel rejected and abandoned, hope reminds us we are not alone … We'll make it.
- When we say our final farewell to someone we love, hope in the life beyond gets us through our grief.[10]

The Bible promises that *"those who hope in the Lord will renew their strength. They will soar on wings like eagles: they will run and not grow weary, they will walk and not be faint."*[11] It takes courage to trust God's wonderful gift of hope.

Courage to Be Committed

The Christian leader exhibits courage daily. Just saying you are a Christian takes courage, because you are held accountable for living the "Christian" way. It takes courage to stand for your values and put yourself in a position to be criticized. Anytime your values conflict with the world's values, you will be criticized. Peter understood the courage required to carry the cross, saying, *"Dear friends, do not be surprised at the painful trial you are suffering, as though something strange were happening to you. But rejoice that you participate in the sufferings of Christ, so that you may be overjoyed when His glory is revealed. If you are insulted because of the name of Christ, you are blessed, for the Spirit of glory and of God rests on you."*[12] Paul also spoke of the courage required to carry the cross: *"For God did not give us a spirit of timidity, but a spirit of power, of love, and of self discipline. So don't be ashamed to testify about our Lord ..."*[13] We may suffer by following the biblical principles outlined in this book. Peter instructed us to endure: *"So then those who suffer according to God's will should commit themselves to their faithful Creator and continue to do good."*[14]

It is not easy to accept that sometimes God uses our suffering for His glory and our prosperity. I know of a man who agonized through a value clash but had the courage to choose to protect his integrity, regardless of the cost. This person, Don, was a man of faith and strong beliefs. He worked for an appraisal company in the Southwest. Don's job was to provide property appraisals based on recent sales in the area and based on his knowledge of the market. He was good at his job and enjoyed what he was doing. When the real estate market was going through a slow period, his boss pressured him to appraise high or low, depending on the situation. Don was to follow those directions or potentially lose his job. This is the real world—a conflict in values, a bad time to be looking for a job, and enjoying your work until you have to make a decision to do what is right or do what you are told to do.

Don is a man of more courage, integrity, and faith than most. He decided that he would not sacrifice his integrity for any reason. Don refused to manipulate his appraisals, so he quit his job. He stepped out in faith and began his own appraisal company, even though his market timing could not have been much worse. Inflation was rampant, and the risk of starting a new business was high. After struggling through the start-up, his business prospered. His company is now successful and is based on the values that he would not sacrifice in his previous job. Don knew that he really did not have a choice. His choice was made when he chose the values by which he would live his life. His courage was in living his commitment to himself and God.

Not every example of courage ends in a financial success story like Don's. In fact, many successful people have not been financially blessed. *The true measurement of success is being able to look in the mirror and know that you had the courage to do what you felt was God's will for your life.* The Bible teaches us the ultimate reward for having such courage: *"So do not throw away your confidence; it will be richly rewarded. You need to persevere so that when you have done the will of God, you will receive what he has promised."*[15] It takes courage to seek the will of God for your life and even more courage to act upon His will.

To develop the courage to be different from the world requires you to have an undeniable, indisputable, unwavering commitment to Christ. A commitment that is dependent upon the circumstance, not on our values, leads to decisions founded on the consequences of our choice rather than our commitment to do what is right. Moses had an unwavering commitment to do what was right, even though it was against his human nature. In the New Testament, Moses was described as a person who *"chose to be mistreated along with the people of God rather than to enjoy the pleasures of sin for a short time."*[16] We have to make the same decision—are the pleasures of sin worth my sacrifice of living for Christ? The short-term pleasures of sin are disastrous to our daily walk with God and the Christian influence we have on others. *A truly committed Christian does not have to weigh the consequences before making a decision. Because of his crystal clear values, the decision was made when he committed his all to Christ.*

Becoming a Courageous Leader

In summary, it takes courage to "carry your cross" while being a leader at work. Conforming to your workplace environment probably will not lead to your ultimate goal of others seeing Jesus in you. Experience the joy of having the courage to get the cross out of your pocket, lean your ladder on the building of God's principles, and keep climbing. More than twenty times Jesus commanded, "Fear not." It takes courage to trust Jesus when we are afraid, unsure, and not confident in ourselves.

Finding the nearest person to blame or being complacent about the way things have always been does not take courage. You can be a courageous leader by deciding to do the following:

1. Depend on God to provide you the courage to lead.
2. Determine the values in your life that cannot be compromised, and develop an unwaivering commitment to those values.
3. Seek the truth, even when the truth might be difficult to accept.
4. Reject the cynics by confronting, training, and setting an optimistic example.
5. Admit when you are wrong and apologize. Keep an eye out on your ego, which tends to separate us from God.
6. Face your criticism. Don't be disabled because you are afraid to be criticized.
7. Focus on hope.
8. Keep your faith.

Miguel de Cervantes once said, "He who loses wealth loses much; he who loses a friend loses more; but he who loses courage loses all." You cannot be an effective leader by conforming to the method of least resistance. *Christian leadership requires courage from the leader, trust from the follower, and direction from the Father.*

> *Do not pray for tasks equal to your powers. Pray for powers equal to your tasks.*
> —*Phillips Brooks*

GENERAL COLIN POWELL'S RULES

1. It ain't as bad as you think. It will look better in the morning.

2. Get mad, then get over it.

3. Avoid having your ego so close to your position that, when your position falls, your ego goes with it.

4. It can be done!

5. Be careful what you choose. You may get it.

6. Don't let adverse facts stand in the way of a good decision.

7. You can't make someone else's choices. You shouldn't let someone else make yours.

8. Check small things.

9. Share credit.

10. Remain calm. Be kind.

11. Have a vision. Be demanding.

12. Don't take counsel of your fears or naysayers.

13. Perpetual optimism is a force multiplier.

CHAPTER TWELVE

EXAMPLE

In everything set them an example by doing what is good.

— Titus 2:7

THE PRINCIPLE OF EXAMPLE

Leadership results improve when the leader provides a positive role model for his followers.

C arl Messina of The Memory Training Institute shares the following poem with his workshop participants:

SHOW ME

I'd rather see a sermon, than hear one any day.
I'd rather you would walk with me, than merely show the way.
The eye's a better pupil, and more willing than the ear,
fine counsel is confusing but example's always clear.
And best of all the preachers, are the men who live their creeds.
For to see good put in action is what everybody needs.
I soon can learn to do it, if you'll let me see it done.
I can see your hands in action, but your tongue too fast may run.
And the lectures you deliver may be very fine and true.
But I'd rather get my lesson observing what you do.
For I may not understand you and the high advice you give.
But there is no misunderstanding how you act and how you live.

(Author Unknown)

Your example of how you live communicates your values far more clearly than any words you may speak. *People follow people.* People do not follow speeches, memos, mission statements, or state-of-the-business reports. People follow people. The question is not, "Are people watching?" The question is, "What are the people seeing?" The principal source of learning in any organization is the observation of other people's behavior. Whether you like it or not, your example has a positive or negative influence on your followers and all the people they influence.

What Does the Bible Say?

After Jesus washed the feet of His disciples, He told them how they should lead by example and told them what the results of their obedience would be. *"I have set you an example that you should do as I have done for you. I tell you the truth, no servant is greater than his master, nor is a messenger greater than the one who sent him. Now that you know these things, you will be blessed if you do them."*[1] We will be blessed if we follow Jesus' example.

The Golden Rule states that we should treat others the way we would want them to treat us: *"So in everything, do to others what you would have them do to you."*[2] This direction is to be proactive, treating others well, not waiting and reacting to a situation. In everything, meet the needs of others as we expect our needs to be met.

Jesus spoke to the Pharisees about the negative influence they had on others: *"Woe to you experts in the law, because you have taken away the key to knowledge. You yourselves have not entered, and you have hindered those who were entering."*[3] Not only were the Pharisees making erroneous interpretations of law, but their example was keeping others away from the truth. At a different time Jesus instructed the disciples to leave the Pharisees alone: *"Leave them; they are blind guides. If a blind man leads a blind man, both will fall in a pit."*[4] There are many people in leadership positions today who are blinded to the truths of biblically based leadership.

Jesus also warned of leaders that live in a way inconsistent with their teachings: *"But do not do what they do, for they do not practice what they preach. They tie up heavy loads and put them on men's shoulders, but they themselves are not willing to lift a finger to move them."*[5] Your ability to lead depends on how committed you are and the actions you choose to take. You can never not lead!

James, the brother of Jesus, wrote, *"Who is wise and understanding among you? Let him show it by his good life, by deeds done in the humility that comes from wisdom."*[6] Your wisdom is illustrated by the example you set for others to follow.

Paul taught the Corinthians the true meaning of setting an example: *"I urge you to imitate me."*[7] Think about that! How much power and accountability would we have if we told everyone to imitate us? **What kind of leadership would exist if everyone imitated biblically based leaders?** Of course that is not happening today. Remember the survey mentioned in the first chapter? Only 14 percent of leaders are seen as role models by their followers. How far off base are we from what Paul was teaching?

Titus was advised, *"In everything set an example by doing what is good. In your teaching show integrity, seriousness, and soundness of speech that cannot be condemned, so that those who oppose you may be ashamed because they have nothing bad to say about us."*[8] Can you imagine your competitors being ashamed because they have nothing bad to say about you or your company? That is how each share of business can be rightfully yours.

Wow! The Bible does not leave much room for our creative interpretations of leading by example. There are no exceptions when we are dealing with our bad bosses or for times when we are out of town and no one knows us. There are no exceptions when someone has hurt us, when we are angry, or when times are tough. There are no exceptions, period. Give no one anything bad to say about you!

Role Models

The Bible directs us to be a positive example everywhere we go! Our children need positive role models. Parents are faced with the task of dealing with enormous pressures at work and at home. The pressures of time, money, and energy sometimes contribute to creating a role model void. Kids are forced to make adult decisions without being prepared for that responsibility. Making the decision to spend time with our children and provide them a positive role model should be at the top of every parent's priority list.

Recently my church interviewed administrators of elementary, middle, and high schools surrounding our church. Each administrator was asked, "How can our church be of service to your school?" The interviews were independent, and no one knew how any one else responded. Yet the answer was the same at every school—"Spend time with the kids and provide them a role model for their future." Our role as Christian leaders does not begin and end at work or in the church. Equally important is the influence we have in our neighborhoods.

Our workplace needs positive role models. An example of a committed Christian unwilling to sacrifice for the world is Truett Cathy of Chick-fil-A. In a competitive business (fast food), Chick-fil-A has made a stand. Its restaurants will not be open on Sundays. Conventional wisdom says that is ridiculous, because Sunday is a big day for fast food, with huge profits. Cathy's wisdom is his trust in God. For six days his employees work, and on the seventh they rest. Any question about his values? Every Chick-fil-A store has a plaque engraved with this principle: "Associate yourselves only with those people you can be proud of—whether they work for you or you work for them." Truett Cathy is leading by example!

Witnessing at Work

Your example at your work place speaks volumes about your Christian commitment. Sometimes it is hard to evaluate the right time and place for witnessing. Nonbelievers at work are generally not interested in a prayer group or Bible study, but there are other methods to witness for Christ. One way to effectively witness at work is to follow these four steps:

1. *Prepare for the right time.* Know what you believe. If you are unsure about your beliefs, it is doubtful that you will be able to communicate a consistent message when the opportunity does occur. Study your Bible, know your beliefs, and prepare for the time when God will provide you an opportunity to witness. Role play with a friend or spouse, and you will be more confident when the real situation comes along. The Bible says, *"Always be prepared to give an answer to everyone who asks you to give the reason for the hope that you have. But do this with gentleness and respect, keeping a clear conscience, so that those who speak maliciously against your good behavior in Christ may be ashamed of their slander."*[9]

2. *Pray for the nonbelievers and pray that the right time to witness will come along.* Pray consistently and earnestly for the salvation of each individual for whom you have a burden. Lift them up to God by name, and pray that you or another believer will be given the opportunity to witness. Follow the attitude of Samuel: *"As for me, far be it from me that I should sin against the Lord by failing to pray for you."*[10]

3. *Live what you believe.* Your greatest influence on nonbelievers is your behavior at work. If there is no difference between you and a nonbeliever, there is no reason for a nonbeliever to desire Christ. Stay in the Word, in prayer, and filled with the Spirit, and the difference will become obvious.

4. *Wait on God's time to witness.* The more you try to force your beliefs on someone, the more resistant they become. You control only your preparation, your prayers, and your actions. Be consistent and dedicated in those three things, and the time will come for you to share your faith verbally.

Example by Humility

The ability to show sincere humility is one of the most powerful examples you can set. Humility is contrary to our personality. The nature of most leaders is to take charge, which many times results in pride. The humility to respect others' opinions, listen with empathy, and seek the wisdom of your followers is an example that is biblically directed. ***The Christian definition of humility is to be God-focused.*** It is impossible to be arrogant when you keep your focus on God! In Proverbs there are graphic descriptions of the results of pride and humility:

- *"When pride comes, then comes disgrace, but with humility comes wisdom."* (Proverbs 11:2)

- *"Pride only brings quarrels, but wisdom is found in those who take advice."* (Proverbs 13:10)

- *"The fear of the Lord teaches a man wisdom, and humility comes before honor."* (Proverbs 15:33)

- *"Pride goes before destruction, a haughty spirit before a fall."* (Proverbs 16:18)

The New Testament is just as clear about humility:

- *"For everyone who exalts himself will be humbled, and he who humbles himself will be exalted."* (Luke 14:11)

- *"Do not think of yourself more highly than you ought, but rather think of yourself with sober judgement, in accordance with the measure of faith God has given you."* (Romans 12:3)

- *"Do nothing out of selfish ambition or vain conceit, but in humility consider others better than yourselves. Each of you should look not only to your own interests, but also to the interests of others."* (Philippians 2:3-4)

> ***Pride = disgrace, quarrels, and destruction.***
> ***Humility = wisdom, honor, and exaltation.***

Jesus is our example of ultimate humility. *"And being found in appearance as a man, he humbled himself and became obedient to death—even death on a cross!"* Philippians 2:8 The cultivation of humility is essential for the Christian leader, because humility is not often found among non-Christian leaders. Humility is opposed to our nature but is in keeping with Jesus Christ's example.

Leading by Example

There are many other ways to be a positive example. Here are twenty-five ways to lead by example:

1. Always treat others the way they would want to be treated.
2. Return all calls promptly.
3. Be available to anyone who needs your help.
4. Praise in public, criticize in private, and surround your criticism with praise.
5. Never criticize an employee for making a customer happy.
6. Know what you can and cannot change, and act accordingly.
7. Be predictable—do what you say you will do.
8. Be unpredictable in trying new things and motivating people to achieve results.
9. Walk your talk.
10. Admit when you are wrong and apologize.
11. Learn how to say "no" to avoid overcommitting.
12. Be an active listener and take action on what you hear.
13. Help others on the way up the corporate ladder.
14. Trust your employees, or find employees that you can trust.
15. Get your own coffee.
16. Get feedback from all levels of employees and customers.
17. Work smart.
18. Treat all followers fairly and consistently.
19. Develop your staff into a team and never pit them against each other.
20. Smile. It is contagious.
21. Continually look for improvements and fight complacency.

22. Strive to get better every day in your professional, personal, and spiritual life.
23. Embrace change and become a change master.
24. Cultivate family relationships.
25. Develop people by showing confidence in them and allowing them to achieve results their way.

Summary

Leadership inherently demands that you serve as a role model for your followers. You have no choice. The principle-based leader does not ignore or take advantage of that responsibility. Jesus is the ultimate example. Christian leaders are to be humble, treat everyone with dignity and respect, and be compassionate. Christian leaders are to address their followers' needs, be close to their followers, and be servants to their followers. If you are living in the Word and guided by the Holy Spirit, your example will be obvious. "... *The fruit of the spirit is love, joy, peace, patience, kindness, goodness, faithfulness, gentleness and self control.*"[11] Your every action is an example to others. You always lead, and everything counts!

Example is not the main thing in influencing others. It is the only thing.

—*Albert Schweitzer*

How Successful Leaders Carry the Cross

Steven D. Davidson
Attorney
McGuire, Craddock, Strother, & Hale, P.C.

I attempt to carry the cross in my law practice through my actions. It is easy to display Christian symbols and profess Christian beliefs. However, my peers, clients, and opponents will judge my faith primarily on the basis of our day-to-day dealings. Although aggressive negotiation is a critical aspect of my practice, I refuse to compromise my personal integrity for any person or any price.

My best opportunity for sharing my faith is with attorneys and clients with whom I have long-standing relationships. These people recognize that my attitudes and lifestyle are different from many other lawyers, giving me the opportunity to explain my Christian beliefs. Through the years, I have learned that people are always watching—even when I am unaware—to see if my actions are consistent with my words.

My constant goal is to maintain a proper balance among the three major segments of my life: my family, my church, and my career. All three of these roles must be centered around my relationship with Jesus if I am to succeed. Finding this Christ-centered balance is a dynamic process requiring perpetual evaluation and correction. However, with God's help and guidance, I believe I can exercise Christian leadership in each of these critical areas.

CHAPTER THIRTEEN

PREPARATION

It is more blessed to give than to receive.

— Acts 20:35

THE PRINCIPLE OF PREPARATION

Leadership results improve to the extent to which the leader develops himself and his followers.

The leaders of the future will be those who prepare themselves by continuing to learn and improve every day. Today's leaders who choose to rest on their knowledge and do not improve will become followers. You prepare for your future through the choices you make in your personal development and self-management.

In Ephesians, Paul gave counsel to the church on preparing for the challenges of the future. His direction was to know your resources: *"Be strong in the Lord, and put on the full armor of God."*[1]

To read his instruction without understanding the situation Paul was facing does not tell the whole story. Paul was in the midst of trials that we can only attempt to imagine. He was in prison, in solitary confinement, and chained to an armored guard twenty-four hours a day. History tells us that he was most likely chained wrist to wrist and ankle to ankle. The guards were on duty for approximately six hours each shift. As Paul was writing those words, he was no doubt preaching to the guards as he described the armored uniform of the guard chained right beside him.

The armor Paul described for the Christians to equip themselves in preparation for the day of evil included the following:

- The **Belt** represents the truth to defend against the lies of Satan.
- The **Breastplate** represents God's righteousness that protects our hearts and ensures God's approval.
- The **Footgear** represents our readiness to spread the gospel.
- The **Shield** represents our faith, which protects us from Satan's arrows.
- The **Helmet** represents our salvation that protects our minds from doubting God's work.
- The **Sword** represents the word of God to use against Satan.

Each piece of God's armor is there to protect us and prepare us for the battles we will face. Isn't it interesting that Paul did not describe any protection for the backside of the soldier? As long as the soldiers are moving forward, they are protected. If they are running from the opposition, they are unprotected. Any missing piece also leaves us vulnerable to the opposition.

Christians must be just as prepared as the soldiers whom Paul described. Every person is faced with difficult choices, choices that may not have a clear right or wrong answer—or choices that challenge your faith, commitment, and desire to keep going. *The key to making your best decisions is to precisely understand your values.* What is the most important thing—the one thing—that cannot be compromised under any circumstance? Until you know your number-one value, you cannot commit to your number-two, -three, or -four values. Once your values are identified, your choices become clear and are easier for you to make.

Preparing for Personal Development

These twelve tips will help you prepare for the challenges of the future:

1. *Make sure your job is congruent with your values.* According to published surveys, up to 80 percent of working Americans occupy a job that is wrong for them. They are discontented because of a conflict in their values and a conflict with God's will for their lives! *If any area of your job conflicts with your value system and what God wants you to do, you are guaranteed to be miserable, and your employees will be miserable as well.* I'm sure you know extremely intelligent, successful, unhappy people who are facing this value clash. Maybe their job requires constant travel and time away from their family. Money is great, but sons and daughters are greater. These people will never reach their potential until their values align with their actions. Ecclesiastes 5:19-20 says that a person should: *"accept his lot and be happy in his work—this is a gift of God. He seldom reflects on the days of his life, because God keeps him occupied with gladness of heart."* You cannot be happy at work if you are continually experiencing a clash with your values.

   Will Rogers once observed that "in order to succeed, you must know what you are doing, like what you are doing and believe in what you are doing." For you to be successful and happy at work, the answer to these four questions must align with your values:

   a. *How do you feel about your job?* Are you proud of the job you have chosen to do? Do you enjoy telling people what you do? How do you feel about your chosen profession? A passion for your job will create energy and focus for you to lead others. If you are not comfortable sharing with others what you do, you are likely in the wrong job.

   b. *How do you feel about the activities your job requires?* Is the travel too much? Do you have to sacrifice your integrity? Do you enjoy the daily activities? Do you look forward to going to work?

Are the activities aligned with your values? You spend at least eight hours a day at work. If you spend that time doing things that conflict with your value system, you are guaranteed misery.

c. *How do you view your ability to do the job well?* Do you think this is God's direction for your life? Do you feel you can excel at this job? Do you enjoy the challenges to your ability that this job provides? Are you working in your area of excellence? Do you believe in yourself enough to lead others to the unknown? Your confidence in being the best in your chosen profession is a major influence on your success.

d. *How do you feel about the company you work for?* Do the company values align with your personal values? Are you proud of the product you represent? Do you enjoy the people you work for and with? Do you believe your product is a good deal for your customer? If you answered no to any of those questions, begin searching for a company where you can feel good about going to work.

People with the strongest and best-defined values are the most productive. If any of these four areas are incongruent with your values, stress will arrive and your job satisfaction will leave. **You cannot achieve long-term happiness in any job in which your values clash with God's direction for your work.**

2. *Live a balanced life and have a feedback system for knowing when you are out of sync.* The way to help you maintain balance is to have goals for each of the five major areas in your life: professional, personal, physical, spiritual, and emotional. Create an upper control limit (the most time you will spend in this area) and a lower control limit (the least amount of time required to fulfill your goals), and stay within your boundaries. No one lives a perfectly balanced life, so you need to establish goals to prevent you from ignoring one important area because you are too focused on another area of your life. Stay within your boundaries.

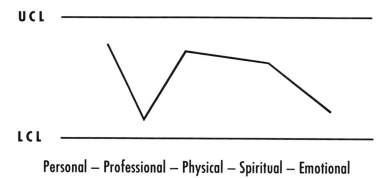

UCL ————————————————————

LCL ————————————————————

Personal – Professional – Physical – Spiritual – Emotional

Personally, I have goals as a spouse (Karen), parent (Jennifer, Kimberly, Michael), son, brother, friend, and alumnus (I love my Razorbacks!). I have physical goals for exercise and golf. I have spiritual goals as a sixth-grade Sunday school teacher and student of the Word. I have professional goals as a leader, follower, and peer. I have emotional goals to make deposits into others' emotional bank accounts and a goal for my self-improvement.

Spending too much time (being above the upper control limit) in any one of these goals will cause me to not spend enough (below the lower control limit) on other important goals. For instance, I could probably be a scratch golfer if I dedicated my time to that goal. Unfortunately, I would have to spend so much time that it would have a negative impact on all my other goals. The price would not be worth it, so my goal is to improve on my current handicap, not to be a scratch golfer.

Balancing your goals is easier to talk and write about than to do. Don't get discouraged; keep working to find the right mix. The first step is to identify each of your roles and write them down. Then establish a monthly goal for each role and the actions necessary to accomplish that goal. Do this for two months and you will see a difference in your satisfaction at work and at home. The following form will help you get started.

BALANCE GOAL PLANNER

Month _____

ROLE	GOALS	ACTIONS
Personal • • • • • •		
Professional • • • •		
Physical • • •		
Spiritual • • • •		
Emotional • • • •		

3. *Read the Bible, pray, and read something positive in regard to your profession.* Find a consistent time and place to read your Bible. The Bible and our prayer life are the principal means through which God provides us direction. Romans 15:4 tells us that the Bible is our encouragement: *"For everything that was written in the past was written to teach us, so that through endurance and the encouragement of the scriptures we might have hope."* None of our problems are new or unique to us. The Bible teaches about every problem we have experienced, are experiencing, or will experience. Get familiar with the Word in order to have your questions answered. *"Your word is a lamp to my feet and a light for my path."*[2] Keep the light on by having your Bible open!

Pray daily. Get in the habit of consistent prayer communication with God. *"Cast all of your anxiety on Him because He cares for you."*[3] Jesus gave us the example: *"Very early in the morning, while it was still dark, Jesus got up, left the house and went off to a solitary place, where he prayed."*[4] Romans 12:12 instructs us to *"be joyful in hope, patient in affection, faithful in prayer."* Jesus prayed for himself, His followers, and all the people touched by His followers. That is a great blueprint of prayer for all leaders. James 5:16 tells us that the *"prayer of a righteous man is powerful and effective."* Find the time to dedicate yourself to prayer.

Read something positive in regard to your profession. There are hundreds of books to help you become more satisfied and productive in your chosen profession. According to Brian Tracy, less than 50 percent of adults read a complete nonfiction book after their last year of formal education. With the amount of information available to us to improve, that is a tragedy! We choose our profession and then choose not to invest our time to learn as much as we can to do our best. What if your doctor told you he had not read any medical journals or attended any seminars since medical school? How long would it take for you to get out of that office? Why should it be any different in your chosen field?

Whatever role you have chosen, make the choice to be the best in that profession. Reading one hour per day for three to five years will make you an expert in any area you choose. You may not have an hour a day to invest, but you can invest 10, 20, or 30 minutes every day. By reading just one book a month, you can join the top one percent in the nation in your chosen profession.

One of the keys to a satisfying life is to be willing to learn and to make a commitment to continue learning. Learn from the Bible, from your prayer life, and from reading within your profession. School is never out of session for the Christian professional. The more you learn, the greater your chances for a prosperous and satisfying career.

4. *Listen to audiotapes.* The average person spends more than 500 hours per year in his car—the equivalent of 12 forty-hour weeks. Turn half of that time into a learning experience, and you create more time for your and your family. Audiotapes are available to educate and motivate you in your spiritual, professional, and personal life. The more productive you are during your "drive time," the better prepared you will be to face the challenges of the day. Don't waste your 500 hours listening to things that do not provide you a benefit.

5. *Go to seminars or take courses.* There are hundreds of low-cost seminars to help you to sharpen your skills. Check your church or local library for some video-based seminars that you can experience. To be refreshed and learn new ideas, go to a full-day seminar or three-day school, such as CornerStone's. Invest in your growth. The return on your investment is self-esteem and job satisfaction. In Colossians 3:23 we are directed, *"Whatever you do, work at it with all your heart, as working for the Lord, not for men."* The disciples knew how important it was to keep learning. They learned by experiencing God's wonders. They learned by their mistakes and by asking Jesus to keep teaching them. Stay on top of the changes in your profession, and keep getting better every day.

6. *Surround yourself with positive people.* Pick one or two ambitious people that you admire who are positive and fun. Meet with them once a week—just to talk. This is a good accountability system for you and will help you keep your sanity when you need to just talk things out. Paul said in Hebrews 10:25, *"Let us not give up meeting together, as some are in the habit of doing, but let us encourage one another— and all the more as you see the day approaching."* Paul also taught the Roman church that *"I long to see you so that I may impart to you some spiritual gift to make you strong—that is, that you and I may be mutually encouraged by each other's faith."*[5] In Ecclesiastes 4:10 we read about positive friends: *"If one falls down, his friend can help him up. But pity the man who falls and has no one to help him up."* You need other people to support you, and other people need you to support them. Having a Christian friend to whom you can relate and be yourself with is important to your mental health. Pick a friend, find the time, choose the place, and lift each other's spirits.

7. *Speak in public.* Just like Moses, most people say that one of the greatest fears they have is speaking in public. Surveys have discovered that people are more afraid of public speaking than dying. Jerry Seinfeld once said, "That means at a funeral, you're better off in the coffin than giving the eulogy." The way to overcome the fear is to attack it. Speak in public often! Public speaking is the single greatest differentiator between candidates competing for upper-level management positions. It is to your benefit to consistently speak somewhere in public. Teaching a Sunday school class is excellent training for your workplace. Teaching demands that you prepare, deliver a message, and address questions. It helps develop your confidence to speak in front of larger groups, and it will build your self-esteem. If you are not ready to teach Sunday school, join Toastmasters or another professional organization that prepares you to speak in public.

8. *Teach what you know to others.* You become what you teach. Be a consistent communicator of what you desire to become, and that will be the standard you live. Jesus' last words of instruction were

clear: *"Go and make disciples ... and teach them to obey everything I have commanded you."*[6] When you teach, you not only follow God's direction, but you also create built-in accountability for you in His work.

What about people who do not care to listen? It is difficult to teach people who do not want to learn. The disciples faced the same issue. Jesus told them not to be discouraged by unresponsive people: *"If anyone will not welcome you or listen to your words, shake the dust off your feet when you leave that home or town."*[7] Don't pick green fruit. The time will come when it is ripe to be picked!

9. *Create your own personal goals and mission.* Man without purpose and goals is crippled. You cannot fulfill any dream without first understanding your purpose. It has been said that less than 5 percent of people have personal goals they are actually working to accomplish. Even fewer write their goals and review them periodically. Believe me, any goal you set is better than not having a goal at all. Without clearly defined goals, you are wandering aimlessly like a ship without a rudder. Your personal goals are the rudder for your life; they steer you in the right direction. You will not achieve your purpose without accurately defining what you are trying to accomplish.

Complete this list of your commitments in the five major areas of your life and set goals for your improvement.

PERSONAL LEVELS OF COMMITMENT

1= Not Committed   3 = Somewhat Committed
5 = Totally Committed

- My commitment to Jesus Christ   _____
  My actions to increase my commitment: _____

  _____

  _____

  _____

- My commitment to my family   _____
  My actions to increase my commitment: _____

  _____

  _____

  _____

- My commitment to my followers   _____
  My actions to increase my commitment: _____

  _____

  _____

  _____

- My commitment to my health _____
  My actions to increase my commitment: _____

  _____

  _____

  _____

- My commitment to use my talents to help others _____
  My actions to increase my commitment: _____

  _____

  _____

  _____

The better you define your goals and mission, the more committed you become to their accomplishment. After you have defined, written down, and committed to your goals, involve others by sharing what you are trying to accomplish. People that you care about, trust, respect, and mentor all want to help you achieve your dreams. Let them know your goals so they can encourage you and celebrate with you as you accomplish them.

10. ***Keep yourself physically healthy.*** There is a direct correlation between job satisfaction and physical health. So much time is spent at work that you cannot afford to be miserable at your job. For your sake and that of everyone else, find a job that fits you and you feel that God has provided for you.

Take care of yourself! You have total control of many areas of your health:
- Keep your weight within reason.
- Eat properly.

- Avoid smoking.
- Use alcohol moderately or not at all.
- Exercise regularly.
- Get plenty of sleep.

Jesus taught his disciples the value of physical renewal. When the disciples told Jesus what they had been doing in their ministry, they said they had not even had time to eat. Jesus directed them to *"come with me to a quiet place and get some rest."*[8] We all need vacations to escape the pressures of our daily work. Take time for renewal. Your ability to accept control of the elements of your life that are controllable is key to your physical and mental health.

11. *Keep your sense of humor.* When you stop laughing at yourself, you are taking yourself too seriously. We are all different; we are all unique. Enjoy the differences in personalities within your work group. The Bible says, *"A cheerful heart is good medicine, but a crushed spirit dries up the bones."*[9]

I once saw the sign below which describes some of the possible personality types within any work group. Wouldn't it be nice to leave these options on your voice mail?

Welcome to the Psychiatric Hotline

— If you are obsessive-compulsive, please press 1 repeatedly.
— If you are codependent, please ask someone else to press 2.
— If you have multiple personalities, please press 3, 4, 5, and 6.
— If you are paranoid-delusional, we know who you are and what you want. Just stay on the line until we can trace the call.
— If you are schizophrenic, listen carefully and a little voice will tell you which number to press.
— If you are manic-depressive, it doesn't matter which number you press. No one will answer.

A good sense of humor is a requirement for job satisfaction. Make it a point to laugh at your own human errors. The Bible says to *"not think of ourselves more highly than we should."*[10] People who can laugh at life and enjoy the world around them are healthier and happier. To develop a sense of humor, try these three ideas:

a. *Always search for the absurdity in difficult situations.* Isn't it strange that after a particularly stressful situation you can look back and see something absurd about it? It is easy in hindsight, but watch for it when you are in the midst of the situation. Healthy and happy people do not experience less stress, but they have figured out a way to cope with the stress they are encountering. They have figured out that—most of the time—you will eventually be able to look back on this crisis and laugh. You might as well look for the reason to laugh now.

b. *Take yourself lightly while taking your work seriously.* Take control of what you can control—your actions, reactions, and attitude. Do your work, but don't do yourself in while doing it.

c. *Have a sense of joy in being alive and healthy.* We are all God's children with a unique purpose for being here. Enjoy the ride!

Use your sense of humor to make life fun!

12. *Keep your faith.* How easy it is to lose our faith. Even the disciples, who saw Jesus perform miracles firsthand, lost their faith. Think of some of the astonishing things they witnessed:

- Five thousand people fed with five loaves and two fish[11]
- Jesus' command over the winds and sea[12]
- Demons transferred from a man into pigs[13]
- The sick healed[14]
- The paralyzed made to walk[15]
- Lepers healed[16]
- Jesus walking on water[17]

- Blind men gaining sight[18]
- Mute men beginning to speak[19]
- Dead men coming back to life[20]
- Water turned to wine[21]
- A man's ear restored[22]
- A lame man healed[23]

After seeing Jesus perform many of those miracles, you would think their faith would never waiver. However, the twelve men who were closest to Jesus still had little faith. No wonder we have to work so hard at growing in our faith. I know how difficult it is to have the faith to keep going when things are tough. I have seen God provide for me when only His divine intervention could explain why certain things happen. Yet when times are tough, I tend to lose faith in the one who has always provided. The only way I know to grow my faith is for me to grow spiritually through the Word and prayer and let God provide in His way with His timing. The Bible says, *"Without faith it is impossible to please God."*[24]

Does God Answer Prayer?

We must possess the faith to know that God is listening to our prayers. Sometimes we lose our patience while waiting on God's answers. Dr. John Bisagno of First Baptist, Houston, Texas, preached a sermon on how God answers prayers that has been an inspiration to me for more than twenty years. All prayers are answered, but they may be answered differently. According to Dr. Bisagno, God answers prayer in one of four ways:

- *Slow.* The timing is not right. You may have prepared all of your life for the opportunity and you are ready, but the timing is not right for you, from God's perspective. Be still and wait on the Lord. *"There is a time for everything, and a season for every activity under heaven."*[25] Keep yourself prepared for when the timing is right.

- *Grow.* The timing is right, the job is available, but you are not right. You need to grow before the situation is right for you. Commit yourself to the improvement needed for the next opportunity. *"Show me your ways, O Lord, teach me your paths, guide me in your truth and teach me, for you are my God and my Saviour, and my hope is in you all day long."*[26] Keep growing until God opens the right door for you.

- *No.* The timing is not right, and you are not right. Too many times we try to fit a round peg into a square hole. The timing is not right; we are not right—so we should pick up and move on. *"Blessed is the man who finds wisdom, the man who gains understanding."*[27] Understand that even if the situation appears fantastic, if you are not right and the timing is not right, the worst result you could experience is to get what you were praying for.

- *Go.* When the timing is right and you are right, you know it. You have peace; you look forward with optimism. No one has to tell you that this opportunity is the right one—you know it! Thank God and enjoy! *"Then I heard the voice of the Lord saying, 'Whom shall I send? And who will go for us?' And I said, 'Here am I. Send me!'"*[28] Be ready to go when the timing is right and you are right!

Hebrews 10:35 teaches us to keep our faith: *"So do not throw away your confidence; it will be richly rewarded. You need to persevere so that when you have done the will of God, you will receive what he has promised."* It takes courage to persevere and demonstrate faith in God to provide what he has promised. Never give up! Keep your faith in God and the direction He has given your life.

Committing to these twelve actions will help you prepare for the future and keep yourself motivated while you are motivating others.

> *If you employed study, thinking, and planning time daily, you could develop and use the power that can change the course of your destiny.*
>
> *—W. Clement Stone*

IF I HAD MY LIFE TO LIVE OVER

I would have talked less and listened more.

I would have invited friends over to dinner
even though the carpet was stained and the sofa was faded.

I would have eaten popcorn in the "good" living room and worried less
about the dirt when someone wanted to light a fire in the fireplace.

I would have burned a pink candle sculpted like a rose
before it melted in storage.

I would have sat on the lawn with my children
and not worried about grass stains.

I would have cried and laughed less while watching television
and done more of it while watching life.

I would have shared more of the responsibilities carried by my wife.

I would have gone to bed when I was sick instead of worrying that the earth
would go into a holding pattern if I missed work for one day.

I would never buy anything just because it was practical,
wouldn't show soil or was guaranteed to last a lifetime.

There would have been more "I love you," more "I am sorry" … but
mostly, given another shot at life, I would seize every moment,
look at it and really see it and live it
—and never give it back.

– Anonymous

THE INVESTMENT PRINCIPLES CHECKUP

• **Empowerment**   • **Courage**   • **Example**   • **Preparation**

PERSONAL RATING   1 (low) — 5 (high)

1. I spend my time in my areas of excellence.   _____
2. I hire people with talents different from my talents.   _____
3. I have the courage to make necessary adjustments.   _____
4. I have the courage to seek the truth.   _____
5. I have the courage to reject cynics.   _____
6. I lead by example.   _____
7. I return calls promptly.   _____
8. My job is congruent with my values.   _____
9. I live a balanced life.   _____
10. I read the Bible daily.   _____
11. I laugh at myself.   _____
12. I am physically healthy.   _____
13. I teach what I know to others who are interested.   _____
14. I speak in public.   _____
15. I communicate with my personal accountability group.   _____
16. I have the patience to wait on God's answer.   _____

Three Areas I Commit to Improve:	My Actions to Improve
1.	1.
2.	2.
3.	3.

THE ULTIMATE VICTORY

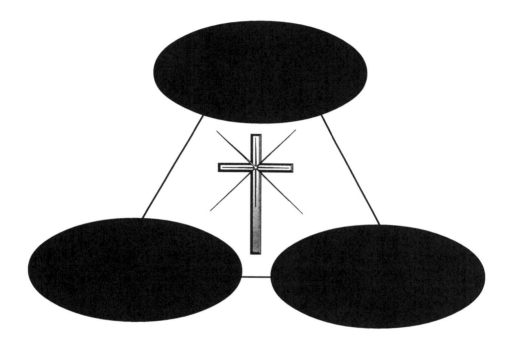

CHAPTER FOURTEEN

THE ULTIMATE VICTORY

Leap for joy, because great is your reward in heaven.

— Luke 6:23

Leadership cannot be claimed with a claim check. It cannot be bought with silver or gold. It cannot be inherited with the writing in a will. It cannot be given to you as a present. It cannot be stolen from someone else that has it. It cannot be made by a manufacturer. It cannot be accepted when you are promoted.

Leadership is earned!

- By living the principles taught in the Bible and expressed in this book
- By maintaining your integrity regardless of the situation you are facing
- By accepting responsibility for all you control
- By surrounding yourself with committed followers
- By having a guiding vision for others to follow
- By communicating with crystal clear clarity
- By solving problems that inhibit your people
- By being optimistic and looking for the best in others
- By empowering others to do what they do best
- By making change positive
- By having the courage to do what's right
- By leading by your example
- By preparing yourself and your people for the future

Your ultimate success as a leader will not be judged by quarterly reports, promotions, money, or recognition. Your influence is far greater than you will ever be able to comprehend.

The average person comes in contact with thousands of people in his or her lifetime. You influence people even when you are not aware that anyone is watching. *You affect others and you do make a difference!* Think of the people who have made a difference in your life.

Remember that Sunday school teacher who helped influence your life? Hundreds of kids participated in her class over the years, and the teacher probably had no idea the positive impression she made on you. Her impact cannot be measured by any report that was generated through the church.

Remember the teacher in school who exhibited the fruits of the Spirit and whom you wanted to emulate? That teacher seldom learns about the positive difference he made in you and the way he helped change your life. There was no report at school that measured what really mattered.

Remember the pastor who was so eloquent in the pulpit, yet took the time to get to know you personally? He helped shape your life with both his words and his actions. There is no report at the church that measured the impact he made on your life.

Remember the secretary who led the Bible study at work on Thursday mornings and consistently prayed for the business and the people in the company? Remember how she ministered and soothed the pain when fellow employees were going through a tragedy that could not be explained? There is no report that measured the impact she made on the lives of others.

The traditional ways of measuring success and effectiveness do not measure long-term impact. The Sunday school teacher's effectiveness might have been measured by attendance each Sunday. The schoolteacher's effectiveness might have been measured by grades the students earned. The Bible study leader might have been measured at work by how quickly and accurately reports were distributed. The pastor's effectiveness might have been measured by church growth. None of those important people were measured by the impact they had on *your* life. If they had been only concerned only with attendance, grades, reports, and church growth, they would not have cared about the difference they had made in the lives of others. Fortunately, they did care. They looked beyond the normal measurements and went out of their way to make a positive influence on you.

Your leadership cannot be measured just by the bottom line. Although that is important, your ultimate victory will come when you are rewarded in ways far beyond what you can imagine. Set your leadership goals and pay the price to accomplish them, but remember that *the ultimate success of the Christian leader will not be measured by any report here on earth.*

What good is success if you lose your family? What good is success without Christ? *"For no one can lay any foundation other than the one already laid, which is Jesus Christ. If any man builds on this foundation using gold, silver, costly stones, wood, hay, or straw, his work will be shown for what it is."*[1] If you judge success by accumulation of money, you are measuring against what the Bible says is meaningless: *"Whoever loves money never has money enough; whoever loves wealth is never satisfied with his income. This too is meaningless."*[2]

Don't get me wrong. Money does not destroy people. There are many Christians who are blessed financially and are living in God's will. In fact, 1 Timothy 5:8 clearly expresses the importance of providing for our families: *"If anyone does not provide for his relatives, and especially for his immediate family, he has denied the faith and is worse than an unbeliever."* However, Jesus talked about money in His parables more than any other subject. Sixteen of Christ's thirty-eight parables dealt with money. Christ knew the temptations that come with money. My point is that measuring man's success just by the money he has accumulated is a false and temporary measurement. Paul instructed Timothy to teach those that are rich to *"not be arrogant or put their hope in wealth, which is so uncertain, but put their hope in God, who richly provides us everything for our enjoyment."*[3]

There is no success without Christ! *"It is required that those who have been given a trust must prove faithful ... it is the Lord who judges me ... He will bring to light what is hidden in darkness and will expose the motives of men's hearts. At that time each will receive his praise from God."*[4] In Ecclesiastes, Solomon wrote about enjoying life while understanding our purpose in life. His conclusion was, *"Fear God and keep his commandments, for this is the whole duty of man. For God will bring every deed into judgement, including every hidden thing, whether it is good or evil."*[5] Our success comes in bringing glory to God.

Effective leadership involves excellence in all of the principles mentioned in this book. All are important, but there are four absolute non-negotiables to your leadership success:

1. *Your Integrity.* There is no reason to sacrifice your integrity that is worth the price. No reason! Your most precious leadership gem is your integrity, and it is measured only by your actions. Two things that we control completely are our integrity and our behavior. Guard your integrity as you would the most precious gem in a vault!

2. *Surround Yourself with Positive, Talented People.* Jethro's advice to Moses is just as applicable to us today. Surround yourself with others whom you trust and who share the same values. The cost of having people on your team whom you do not trust can be more detrimental to your success than any single action of a competitor. Surround yourself with trustworthy, talented, God-loving people, and their skill will bring success.

2. *Communicate Clearly and Often.* Keeping people informed is the most effective way to release employees' stress and earn their trust. People can react to what they know and make plans to deal with

the situation. Always err on the side of overcommunicating. Positive and effective communication involves treating everyone with dignity and respect, listening to and acting on your employees' needs, and being clear about the direction in which you are leading.

Make communication with your heavenly Father a priority! Read, study, pray—never stop communicating.

3. *Keep Growing.* Your spiritual and professional growth is critical to your physical and mental health. Things change too rapidly to go into a learning hibernation. Keep getting better every day. Your prayer and study time is the greatest return on your time investment that you can make. Jesus always prayed before every significant event in his life. He taught us how to handle life's crises by prayer and submission to God's will. The more you experience faith through trials, the easier it is to trust God to provide all of your needs and to experience the joy of knowing that God is in control!

My final note is to remind you of the ultimate non-negotiable of life. Your decision to be a follower of Jesus Christ and a leader in bringing others to Christ is the most important decision you will ever make. Jesus said, *"By their fruit you will recognize them."*[6] Our fruit is displayed by applying what we know and having others see Jesus in us wherever we are.

Rudyard Kipling wrote a poem describing what will happen if all Christians leave their crosses in their pockets and lean their ladders on the wrong buildings:

> They shut the road through the woods
>> Seventy years ago.
> Weather and rain have undone it again
>> And now you would never know
> There once was a road through the woods.
>
>> — *Rudyard Kipling*

David spoke of the shortness of our lives in Psalms: *"As for man, his days are like grass, he flourishes like a flower of the field; and the wind blows over it and it is gone, and its place remembers it no more."*[7] The Christian influence on society will be washed out like an eroded road and blown away like a flower in the field unless Christians replace the liberal teachings of television and the media with biblically based leadership.

If we Christian leaders take the crosses out of our pockets and lean our ladders on God's building, our children will grow up in godly homes, our students will live by Christian values, our business associates will see integrity, our churches will experience committed followers, and everyone will see Jesus in us. That is what really counts! Our ultimate victory will come when we are face to face with the Father and He tells us, *"Well done, thy good and faithful servant."* I can hardly wait!

Best wishes for your successful leadership while carrying the cross.

May the God of Peace, who through the blood of the eternal covenant brought back from the dead our Lord Jesus, that great shepherd of the sheep, equip you with everything good for doing his will, and may he work in us what is pleasing to him through Jesus Christ, to whom be glory for ever and ever. Amen.

Hebrews 13:20

APPENDIX

THE PRINCIPLES OF SUCCESSFUL LEADERSHIP

Principle #1—THE PRINCIPLE OF INTEGRITY

My lips shall not speak wickedness, nor my tongue utter deceit.
> — *Job 27:4*

Leadership results improve in proportion to the level of trust earned by the leader.

Principle #2—THE PRINCIPLE OF RESPONSIBILITY

From everyone who has been given much, much will be demanded; and from the one who has been entrusted with much, much more will be asked.
> — *Luke 12:48*

Leadership results improve dramatically when the leader and his followers accept total responsibility for their actions.

Principle #3—THE PRINCIPLE OF COMMITMENT

Whoever wants to be great among you must be your servant, and whoever wants to be greatest of all must be the slave of all.
> — *Mark 10:43-44 (LB)*

Leadership results improve to the extent that the leader respects, recognizes, and develops his or her committed followers.

Principle #4—THE PRINCIPLE OF VISION

Where there is no vision, the people perish.
> — *Proverbs 29:18 (KJV)*

Leadership results improve when leaders communicate a crystal clear vision and a convincing reason for accomplishing the vision.

Principle #5—THE PRINCIPLE OF COMMUNICATION

Do not let any unwholesome talk come out of your mouths, but only what is helpful for building others up according to their areas, that it may benefit those who listen.

— Ephesians 4:29

Leadership results improve when followers understand their role and are rewarded for their accomplishments.

Principle #6—THE PRINCIPLE OF CONFLICT RESOLUTION

Consider it pure joy, my brothers, whenever you face trials of many kinds, because you know that the testing of your faith develops perseverance.

— James 1:2-3

Leadership results improve to the extent that the leader is able to timely remove the obstacles inhibiting his or her followers.

Principle #7—THE PRINCIPLE OF OPTIMISM

Whatever things are true, whatsoever things are honest, whatsoever things are just, whatsoever things are lovely, whatsoever things are of good report, if there be any virtue, and if there be any peace, think on these things.

— Philippians 4:8

Leadership results improve in direct proportion to the self-concept and optimism of the leader.

Principle #8—THE PRINCIPLE OF POSITIVE CHANGE MANAGEMENT

So they shook their feet in protest against them and went to Iconium. And the disciples were filled with joy and with the Holy Spirit.

— Acts 13:51-52

Leadership results improve to the extent that the leader is able to embrace change and accept responsibility for change.

Principle #9—THE PRINCIPLE OF EMPOWERMENT

Give and it shall be given to you; good measure, pressed down, and shaken together, and running over, shall men give into your bosom.

— *Luke 6:38 (KJV)*

Leadership results improve as followers are provided the opportunity to accept total ownership of their work.

Principle #10—THE PRINCIPLE OF COURAGE

And be not conformed to this world; but be ye transformed by the renewing of your mind, that ye may prove what is that good, and acceptable, and perfect, will of God.

— *Romans 12:2 (KJV)*

Leadership results improve in proportion to the leader's courage to address issues affecting his or her followers.

Principle #11—THE PRINCIPLE OF EXAMPLE

In everything set them an example while doing what is good.

— *Titus 2:7*

Leadership results improve when the leader provides a positive role model for his or her followers."

Principle #12—THE PRINCIPLE OF PREPARATION

It is more blessed to give than to receive.

— *Acts 20:35*

Leadership results improve to the extent to which the leader develops himself and his followers.

INSPIRATIONAL PASSAGES FOR
LEADERS CARRYING THE CROSS

These passages are my favorites for keeping my eyes on the cross.

Psalms 27:14   *Wait on the Lord: be of good courage, and He shall strengthen thine heart.*

1 Peter 4:16   *If you suffer as a Christian, do not be ashamed, but praise God that you bear His name.*

James 1:12   *Blessed is the man who perseveres under trial, because when he has stood the test, he will receive the crown of life that God has promised to those that love Him.*

Philippians 4:10   *I have learned to be content whatever the circumstances.*

Philippians 4:13   *I can do everything through Him who gives me strength.*

Philippians 4:19   *And my God will meet all of your needs according to His glorious riches in Christ Jesus.*

Hebrews 10:36   *You need to persevere so that when you have done the will of God, you will receive what He has promised.*

1 Timothy 6:17   *Command those who are rich in his present world not to be arrogant nor to put their hope in wealth, which is so uncertain, but to put their hope in God, who richly provides us with everything for our enjoyment.*

Proverbs 3:5-6   *Trust in the Lord with all your heart and lean not on your own understanding; in all your ways acknowledge Him, and He will make your paths straight.*

Joshua 1:9 *Have I not commanded you? Be strong and courageous. Do not be terrified, do not be discouraged, for the Lord your God will be with you wherever you go.*

Psalm 127:1 (KJV)*Except the Lord build the house, they labor in vain that build it.*

1 Corinthians 10:13 *No temptation has seized you except what is common to man. And God is faithful; He will not let you be tempted beyond what you can bear. But when you are tempted, He will also provide a way out so that you can stand up under it.*

1 Corinthians 9:24 *Do you know that in a race all the runners run, but only one gets the prize? Run in such a way as to get the prize.*

Galatians 6:8-9 *The one who sows to please his sinful nature, from that nature will reap destruction; the one who sows to please the Spirit, from the Spirit will reap eternal life. Let us not become weary in doing good, for at the proper time we will reap a harvest if we do not give up.*

Philippians 3:13-14 *But one thing I do! Forgetting what is behind and straining toward what is ahead, I press on toward the goal to win the prize for which God has called me heavenward in Christ Jesus.*

2 Timothy 1:12 *That is why I am suffering as I am. Yet, I am not ashamed, because I know whom I have believed, and am convinced that He is able to guard what I have entrusted to Him for that day.*

Psalm 56:3 *When I am afraid, I will trust in you.*

1 Corinthians 16:13   *Be on your guard; stand firm in the faith; be men of courage; be strong. Do everything in love.*

Isaiah 40:31   *But those who hope in the Lord will renew their strength. They will soar on wings like eagles, they will run and not grow weary, they will walk and not faint.*

Psalm 46:1   *God is our refuge and strength, an ever present help in trouble.*

2 Chronicles 26:5 *As long as he sought the Lord, God gave him success.*

Isaiah 54:10   *Though the mountains be shaken and the hills be removed, yet my unfailing love for you will not be shaken nor my covenant of peace be removed, says the Lord, who has compassion on you.*

2 Timothy 2:15   *Do your best to present yourself to God as one approved, a workman who does not need to be ashamed and who correctly handles the word of truth.*

ACKNOWLEDGMENTS

It is impossible to name all of the people whose influence made this book possible. I have been blessed to work with outstanding people at Xerox, FedEx, and the National Spirit Group. I have been blessed by outstanding church leaders. Most important, I have been blessed by Karen, my wife of twenty-two years, and my children—Jennifer, Kimberly, and Michael. I am thankful for all of these pillars of my life.

This book is the accumulation of the efforts of many. My special thanks to my sister Evelyn Addis who spent hours working through my initial manuscript. To my mom and dad, Mary and Ralph Cottrell, for reading every line out loud with me and making suggestions for improvement. And to others who provided input: Betty Ann Bird, Phil Childress, Fred Collins, Hal Habecker, Louis Krueger, Mark Morierity, Fred Roach, Chris Stark, Mark Young, Brian Waite, and Bill White.

The people who have provided encouragement to me through the years: Sherry Barton, Johnny Koons, Kevin Marshall, Joe Miles, Dan Walston, John Winkelman, and especially Tod Taylor.

The Christian leaders who shared their testimony in the book: Ken Byrd, Steve Davidson, Dianne Gibson, Dr. Bob Griggs, and Mark Shackelford.

My business associates who have consistently supported my efforts over the years: Alice Adams, Ken Carnes, Paul Damoc, Bryan Dodge, Mark Layton, Tony Van Roekel, Tom Montgomery, and Robert Kipp.

The people whose expertise made the book a reality: Lynda Pieper—my typist, Defae Weaver—the book designer, Keith Crabtree—the cover designer, and Sue Coffman—my editor.

To all of you whom I have named, please accept my deepest thanks.

To each person who reads this book, best wishes as you become the leader He wants you to be.

David Cottrell

ABOUT THE AUTHOR

David Cottrell is president and CEO of CornerStone Leadership Institute. CornerStone consults and teaches leadership principles and is headquartered in Dallas, Texas.

A nationally known public speaker and business leadership consultant, Cottrell has trained more than 12,000 managers at major corporations and has been a featured expert on public television. He is also the author of *Birdies, Pars, and Bogies: Leadership Lessons from the Links.*

Mr. Cottrell is an active member of First Baptist Church Oak Cliff in Dallas and has taught sixth-grade Sunday school for more than eleven years.

Prior to founding CornerStone, Mr. Cottrell was a senior manager at Xerox and Federal Express. He also led the turnaround of a Chapter 11 apparel company—National Spirit Group.

Mr. Cottrell resides in DeSoto, Texas, with his wife, Karen, and three children—Jennifer, Kimberly, and Michael.

He can be reached at:

> P.O. Box 764087
> Dallas, Texas 75376
> 888-789-LEAD
> www.davidcottrell.com
> d1cottrell@aol.com

A MESSAGE FROM THE AUTHOR

Dear Reader,

It is my sincere desire that the principles expressed in this book will help you become a more effective Christian leader. I believe with all my heart that Christian leaders can make a difference in our society. The purpose of the book was to provide you a guide as you search through the Scriptures for the answers to today's issues.

I would appreciate any comments or suggestions you have about the book. What did you enjoy? What other principles have you discovered that I might share in my seminars or future writings? What suggestions do you have to make the book more effective? I would love to hear from you.

In addition, my desire is for this book to be the vehicle to expose as many people to Jesus Christ as possible. During the next two weeks you will have the opportunity to recommend this book to at least ten friends and associates. It will inspire your Christian friends and reveal the wisdom of the Bible to your associates who do not know Christ. Your recommendation could make a difference!

I hope to hear from you soon. If you write to me, I will send you a gift, so please include your return address.

May God bless you,

David Cottrell

CornerStone's
Eight Keys to Personal Security

1. Keep Your Faith

2. Cultivate Your Family Relationships

3. Have Integrity

4. Develop Your People

5. Master Change

6. Keep Your Sense of Humor

7. Get Better Every Day

8. Enjoy the Victories

CornerStone Leadership Offerings

- Management Development Seminars

  Twelve Principles of Successful Leadership—One- or two-day workshop designed to provide the foundation for effective leadership

  Leadership ... Biblically Speaking—Four-hour to two-day workshop connecting Biblical leadership principles to leadership in the work place. Based on the book *Leadership ... Biblically Speaking*

- Christian Leadership Conferences

  Weekend retreats

  Leadership series

- Management Retreats and Speeches
  Thirty-minute to two-hour presentations available on:
  — Three ways to improve your leadership success
  — Leadership lessons from golf based on *Birdies, Pars, and Bogies: Leadership Lessons from the Links*
  — Principles of leadership
  — Leadership ... Biblically Speaking
  — Eight Keys to Personal Security

  Customer golf outings or sales meetings

  In-house leadership consulting

- Videos, Audios and Workbooks Available — Call 1-888-789-LEAD

REFERENCES

INTRODUCTION — JACUZZIS, LADDERS AND THE CROSS
1 Corinthians 3:19
2 Ephesians 2:10
3 Luke 9:20

CHAPTER ONE — THE CALL FOR LEADERSHIP
1 Exodus 3-4
2 Robert Kelley, *The Power of Followership* (Doubleday, 1992)
3 Ibid.
4 Shipper and Wilson Study, 1996
5 Ibid.
6 Ibid.
7 Robert Kelley, *The Power of Followership* (Doubleday, 1992)
8 Frederick Reichheld, *The Loyalty Effect* (Harvard Business Press, 1996)
9 John C. Maxwell, *Developing the Leader Within You* (Nelson, 1993)
10 Exodus 3:11-4:17
11 Exodus 4:29-31
12 Ecclesiastes 11:4

CHAPTER TWO — INTEGRITY
1 John C. Maxwell, *Developing the Leader Within You* (Nelson, 1993)
2 Genesis 43:12
3 Book of Job
4 Romans 12:21
5 "Disabled by a Paper Cut," *Readers' Digest,* November 1997
6 Romans 7:18-19
7 James 1:12
8 1 Thessalonians 5:22 (KJV)
9 Titus 2:7-8
10 1 Peter 3:14

CHAPTER THREE — RESPONSIBILITY

[1] Hebrews 4:13
[2] Matthew 27:24
[3] Matthew 25:14-30
[4] James 3:1
[5] David Hartley-Leonard, "Perspectives," *Newsweek*, August 24, 1987
[6] Ferdinand Fournies, *Why Employees Don't Do What They Are Supposed To Do* (Liberty Hall Press, 1988)
[7] Stephen Covey, Seven Habits of Highly Effective People (Simon & Schuster, 1990)

CHAPTER FOUR — COMMITMENT

[1] Matthew 9:36
[2] Matthew 15:29-39
[3] Matthew 13:34
[4] Revelation 3:15
[5] 1 Corinthians 12:24-31
[6] Robert Half International Study
[7] Michael Solomon, Ph.D., social psychologist, Graduate School of Business, N.Y.U.
[8] John 13:12-17
[9] Luke 14:11
[10] Mark 12:30
[11] Eugene Habecker, *Leading With A Follower's Heart* (Victor, 1990)
[12] 1 John 2:15
[13] 2 Timothy 3:12
[14] Luke 12:34
[15] Luke 22:42
[16] Galatians 6:2
[17] Mark 8:38

CHAPTER FIVE — VISION

[1] Genesis 12:1-3
[2] Exodus 3:10
[3] Joshua 1:6-3:5
[4] Matthew 6:22-23
[5] Matthew 4:19-20

[6] Luke 4:18

[7] Quoted in Stephen B. Oates, *Let The Trumpet Sound: The Life of Martin Luther King, Jr.* (Harper and Row, 1982)

[8] John C. Maxwell, *Developing The Leader Within You* (Nelson, 1993)

CHAPTER SIX — COMMUNICATIONS

[1] Exodus 3:1-3

[2] Luke 9:23-24

[3] Luke 3:22

[4] Luke 19:17

[5] Richard Hussman and John Hatfield, *Managing The Equity Factor,* (Houghton Mifflin, 1987)

[6] Mark 4:38

[7] Luke 10:40

[8] Mark 10:35-45

[9] Acts 26:16-18

[10] Mark 13:4-23

[11] Matthew 28:19-20

[12] Luke 10:40-42

[13] "Message Madness," *The Dallas Morning News,* July 2, 1997

[14] Luke 18:1

[15] Psalm 46:10

[16] Isaiah 30:15

[17] 1 Thessalonians 5:19

[18] Luke 18:41

CHAPTER SEVEN — CONFLICT RESOLUTION

[1] Proverbs 27:12 (LB)

[2] The Book of Nehemiah

[3] Mark 4:35-41

[4] Proverbs 18:13-17

[5] Genesis 4:1-10

[6] Mark 3:25

[7] Proverbs 23:23 (LB)

[8] Story told in *Managing the Equity Factor,* Hussman and Hatfield (Houghton Mifflin, 1989)

[9] 1 Samuel 30:1-6

CHAPTER EIGHT — OPTIMISM

[1] Matthew 5

[2] Philippians 4:6

[3] Luke 8:9-15

[4] Matthew 6:33

[5] Matthew 11:28-30

[6] Proverbs 22:24-25

[7] 1 Corinthians 15:33

[8] EPC International, Houston, Texas

[9] Adapted from G. W. Target, "The Window," in *The Window And Other Essays* (Mountain View: Pacific Press Publishing Association, 1973), 5-7

CHAPTER NINE — POSITIVE CHANGE MANAGEMENT

[1] Max Dupree, Leadership Is an Art, (Doubleday, 1989)

[2] Exodus 4

[3] Genesis 12

[4] Galatians 6:9

CHAPTER TEN — EMPOWERMENT

[1] James Belasco and Ralph Stayer, *Flight of the Buffalo* (Warner, 1993)

[2] Exodus 18:15-27

[3] Luke 9:1-6

[4] Luke 8:22-53

[5] 2 Timothy 3:10 - 4:6

[6] 1 Peter 4:10

[7] Luke 9:10

CHAPTER ELEVEN — COURAGE

[1] Judges 7

[2] Genesis 6-7

[3] 1 Samuel 17:37

[4] Daniel 3:8-27

[5] Acts 9:23-30

[6] Acts 4:1-4

[7] Acts 9:20

[8] Luke 4
[9] Romans 12:2
[10] Charles Swindoll, *Hope Again,* (Word, 1996)
[11] Isaiah 40:31
[12] 1 Peter 4:12-16
[13] 2 Timothy 1:7
[14] 1 Peter 4:19
[15] Hebrews 10:35-36
[16] Hebrews 11:25

CHAPTER TWELVE — EXAMPLE
[1] John 13:15-17
[2] Matthew 7:12
[3] Luke 11:52
[4] Matthew 15:14
[5] Matthew 23:3-4
[6] James 3:13
[7] 1 Corinthians 4:16
[8] Titus 2:6-8
[9] 1 Peter 3:15-16
[10] 1 Samuel 12:23
[11] Galatians 5:22-23

CHAPTER THIRTEEN — PREPARATION
[1] Ephesians 6:10-17
[2] Psalm 119:105
[3] 1 Peter 5:7
[4] Mark 1:35
[5] Romans 1:11-12
[6] Matthew 28:19-20
[7] Matthew 10:14
[8] Mark 6:30-32
[9] Proverbs 17:22
[10] Romans 12:3
[11] Luke 9:12-17
[12] Luke 8:22-25

[13] Luke 8:26-39

[14] Luke 8:43-48

[15] Luke 5:17-26

[16] Luke 5:12-15

[17] Mark 6:45-52

[18] Matthew 9:27-31

[19] Matthew 9:33

[20] John 11:1-45

[21] John 2:1-11

[22] Luke 22:49-51

[23] John 5:1-16

[24] Hebrews 11:6

[25] Ecclesiastes 3:1

[26] Psalm 25:4-5

[27] Proverbs 3:13

[28] Isaiah 6:8

CHAPTER FOURTEEN — THE ULTIMATE VICTORY

[1] 1 Corinthians 3:11-13

[2] Ecclesiastes 5:10

[3] 1 Timothy 6:17

[4] 1 Corinthians 4:2-5

[5] Ecclesiastes 12:13-14

[6] Matthew 7:16

[7] Psalms 103:15-16